*It always seems impossible until it is done.*

—Nelson Mandela

# The
# ARRIVAL
## *of the*
# ELECTRIC CAR

AN OVERVIEW OF THE EV REVOLUTION HAPPENING NOW
BUYER'S GUIDE, OWNER'S GUIDE, HISTORY, FUTURE

Chris Johnston

Ed Sobey, PhD

ISBN: 978-1-7359294-0-8 (Paperback)

ISBN: 978-1-7359294-1-5 (eBook)

First printing edition 2020

Please contact us at:
info@evpubs.com

This book is dedicated to L and S.

# FOREWORD

Electric vehicles are fascinating. In fact, I'd bet they're just as fascinating to drivers today as they were when the first ones were invented over 100 years ago. I know that this topic doesn't get boring because I've written thousands of articles about EVs over the last decade and a half. I've covered everything from the very beginning of Tesla to the work that the EV activists from Plug In America did to turn California into the EV leader it is today to the slow but steady progress EVs have made towards the mainstream. In fact, let me double down on that bet: I think EVs are more fascinating now than they were a century ago. And everything I've seen points to another 100 years of fascinating, zero-emission rides.

Personally, it's been fascinating to cover advances in electric vehicles for everyone from The New York Times to Car and Driver to blogs dedicated to green transportation. The news never ends, which is exciting. I remember the days when we talked about the first-generation Nissan Leaf being able to go over 100 miles on a charge if the driver was careful and the conditions were right. And now here we are wondering if the 200+ miles in the Polestar 2 will be enough.

Of course it is, but not everyone "gets it" at the same pace. Over the years, I've learned there are three main types of people who develop an interest in EVs, but people can easily fall into multiple categories.

A friend once jokingly called the first group "cashed-up greenies." These are people who are willing and able to spend a bit extra to put their environmental values into action. Especially in the 1990s and 2000s, buying an EV - or converting a gas vehicle to battery power - was an expensive proposition. But these early advocates quickly discovered there was more to driving electric than doing less damage to the environment.

Which is why so many of them joined the second category: the performance folks. It's thrilling to be behind the wheel of an EV, and the first time I drove a Tesla Roadster back in 2008 or so, it blew my little blogger mind. The thrill of instant torque is no joke, and automakers are finally starting to realize this side of EVs in the way they market and sell their vehicles. Looking at you, Porsche Taycan.

Which brings us to the third category: you, i.e., everyone. Yes, despite the prevalence of internal combustion vehicles on the road today, the segment of the population that can afford an EV is growing. Prices are coming down, used EVs are a real option and there are a number of programs in the U.S. focused on getting zero-emission electric vehicles into the hands of average drivers and car shoppers. Two of the big issues that may have kept buyers away in the past, have changed in the last few years. Range is less and less of an issue and more and more body styles are going electric. You can buy plug-in hatchbacks, sedans and SUVs in North America right now, and trucks are coming soon. While this book focuses on the EVs you can buy in North America - where more than two dozen will be on sale in 2021 - the number of EVs available in other parts of the world, including China, is mind boggling. I've rarely been as amazed walking through an auto show as I have in Shanghai or Guangzhou in recent years, where I saw not just a fair number of models I'd never heard of, but entire brands that were new to me. It was, well, fascinating.

Those experiences were also proof that something big is happening. EVs have not seen the constant development that gasoline and diesel vehicles had throughout the 20th Century, thanks to the cheap reliability of fossil fuels and the never-ending challenge of convincing people to try something new. Thankfully, now that the electric vehicle R&D "dark ages" are coming to an end and automakers around the world are charging up their EV programs, there's no doubt that we're about to see massive, valuable change in our transportation landscape.

All signs point to 2021 being a transformational year for EVs. This book is a guide to the fascinating world that's coming. Read it and be ready.

Sebastian Blanco
Freelance Writer
@SebastianBlanco
sebastian-blanco.com

Sebastian Blanco has been writing about electric vehicles since 2006. The New York Times, Forbes, Car and Driver, Automotive News, Reuters, Autoblog, InsideEVs, Trucks.com, and NPR's Car Talk listen to his advice and publish his articles. Since the launch of the Tesla Roadster he has been America's voice tracking the shift away from gasoline-powered vehicles to electric.

# CONTENTS

Foreword..................................................................................vii
Introduction...........................................................................xiii
Why Is the Revolution Happening Now?...............................1
    Price......................................................................................2
    Range...................................................................................4
    Connectivity........................................................................6
    The Importance of Design................................................7
From Birth through Maturation –
    A History of Electric Vehicles........................................13
EV Advantages......................................................................27
    Performance......................................................................29
    Efficiency...........................................................................32
    Lithium-Ion Batteries......................................................33
    Low Cost of Ownership..................................................35
    Reliability..........................................................................39
    What Is Regenerative Braking?......................................40
EV Myths................................................................................45
Electric Vehicle Type Choices..............................................57
    Battery Electric Vehicles.................................................57
    Hybrid Electric Vehicles.................................................58
    Parallel Hybrid..................................................................59
    Series Hybrid or Range-Extended Electric Vehicles...........60
    Plug-In Hybrid Electric Vehicles...................................61
    Hybrids with Lightweight Motors.................................62
    Other Hybrids...................................................................63
    Fuel-Cell Electric Vehicles..............................................63
EV Buying Guide...................................................................67
    Audi e-tron........................................................................68
    BMW i3...............................................................................70
    BMW i4...............................................................................72
    Chevrolet Bolt..................................................................74
    Ford Mustang Mach-E.....................................................76

Hyundai Ioniq Electric .................................................. 78
Hyundai Kona Electric ................................................. 80
Jaguar I-PACE ............................................................. 82
Kia Niro EV ................................................................. 84
Lordstown Endurance .................................................. 86
Lucid Air ..................................................................... 88
Mercedes-Benz EQC ................................................... 90
MINI Cooper Electric ................................................... 92
Nissan Ariya ............................................................... 94
Nissan LEAF ............................................................... 96
Polestar 2 ................................................................... 98
Porsche Taycan ........................................................ 100
Rivian R1T ................................................................ 102
Rivian R1S ................................................................ 104
Tesla Model S ........................................................... 106
Tesla Model X ........................................................... 108
Tesla Model 3 ........................................................... 110
Tesla Model Y ........................................................... 112
Tesla Roadster 2.0 ................................................... 114
Tesla Cybertruck ...................................................... 116
Volkswagen ID.4 ....................................................... 118
Notable Exceptions ................................................... 120
Owning an EV ................................................................ 123
Charging .................................................................. 123
Cost to Charge ......................................................... 130
Tax Credits and Incentives ....................................... 131
Warranty .................................................................. 132
Insurance ................................................................. 132
Future ............................................................................ 133
Accelerating Innovation ............................................ 134
Government Mandates .............................................. 136
Modernized Power Grid and Renewable Energy ........... 138
Electric Motorcycles ................................................. 142
The Commercial Segment .......................................... 142
Technical Definitions and Explainers ............................. 145
About the Authors ......................................................... 151
End Notes ..................................................................... 153
Photo Attribution .......................................................... 161

# INTRODUCTION

When Chris first sat in an electric car, it was clear that it had not been designed in Detroit or Bavaria. It was clean and modern looking but also comfortable and inviting. During the first drive, he was delighted by the silence and how well he could hear the stereo. Most of all, he was shocked by the acceleration.

It wasn't just the acceleration, but the instant response—something that you simply don't experience in a gasoline-powered car due to mechanical lag. He felt much more in control because of how smoothly it accelerated and how well the power steering responded.

Now, after two years of owning it, he still looks forward to every drive. The transition from his beloved gas-powered car to his electric vehicle (EV) brought to mind the change from using a Blackberry's keyboard to an iPhone screen. At first, there was a little apprehension, but after a day, there was no way he was going back to the old phone.

Now, the thought of having to go back to gas stations or to the hassle of oil changes makes him cringe like the thought of having to go from a smartphone back to a flip phone. Many EV owners tell the same story.

They tell us the price is right. The driving range isn't a concern. They love the modern design. They've made the switch, and they aren't going back.

All of us are witnessing a once-in-a-lifetime transformation. For over one hundred years, gasoline and diesel fuels have powered ground transportation throughout the world. Now that is changing, and 2021 is the year when most people will recognize that change is happening.

We wrote this book to share our excitement and what we have learned about electric vehicles. Our goal is to be objective, non-political, and data-driven. What would you expect from authors who are an engineer and a scientist?

Although we describe EV variants like hybrid electric vehicles (HEV) and fuel-cell electric vehicles (FCEV), this buyer's guide is focused on the North American mass market for battery electric vehicles (BEV), also referred to as "pure EVs." In 2020 and prior, there were a handful of EVs on the North American market. With more than twenty-five mass-market electric vehicles from which to choose, 2021 promises to be a breakout year.

# WHY IS THE REVOLUTION HAPPENING NOW?

Why are electric vehicles finally having their moment in the sun? Products achieve mass adoption when they have overcome major consumer objections. In the case of electric vehicles, there were three major objections: price, range, and design. As we will discuss below, all three of these objections have been satisfied, and that has opened the flood gates of consumer demand.

Regarding EVs having their moment, one proof point is that in Q4 of 2019, the Tesla Model 3 had an estimated 26 percent market share in the small and midsize luxury car category. This category includes twenty-six cars, such as the BMW 3 Series, Audi A3, Lexus ES, and the Volvo 90 series.

A 26 percent market share means that one in four cars sold in the category was a Tesla Model 3. What's more, during the first quarter of 2020, the Tesla Model 3 became the number one selling car in California. It displaced the much cheaper

Honda Civic from the top spot. These are stunning achievements that are, for some reason, not widely reported.

## PRICE

To achieve an attractive price, manufacturers must drive down major costs. The two main cost drivers in making electric vehicles are the batteries and low manufacturing volume. Over the last fifteen years, battery costs have consistently dropped, to the extent that most EVs can now be competitively priced in the mid-market luxury range. It hasn't yet been possible to price at the economy-car level, but cost curves show that it will be possible within the next few years. Some automakers have already announced an intent to enter the economy market.

In 2010, the cost of lithium-ion batteries per kWh was $1,000. By 2019, that cost had fallen to $156 per kWh, and it continues to fall. A cost of $100 per kWh is widely agreed to be the figure where EVs and internal-combustion engine (ICE) vehicles will have a comparable upfront purchase price.

---

### Under the Hood

*One measure of a battery's utility is how much energy it can hold. Electrical energy is measured in kilowatt-hours. The electric meter at your home uses this same measure. If you have ten 100-watt light bulbs turned on for one hour, you have used one kilowatt-hour of energy. We use a shorthand for these units, kWh.*

---

The cost of batteries for EVs has fallen year to year since 2010. We project that the cost will continue to fall.

The other challenge for electric vehicle manufacturers has been reaching critical levels of production to achieve an attractive economy of scale. With its LEAF, Nissan showed that it was a possibility. With its Model 3 reaching production volumes of almost 50,000 units per quarter, Tesla proved it in late 2019.

The Nissan LEAF

Production levels present a chicken and egg scenario. More people will purchase EVs when the cost drops, and the cost will drop when more people buy them. We are at the historic point—the critical point for production—when sales are strong enough to allow more cost-efficient production.

## RANGE

EV range is how far the vehicle can drive on a charge. Without any radical advancements in technology, EV range has steadily improved over the last ten years.

We estimate that average range will double in the next five to seven years and will continue to improve after that. Nissan has had historic range expansion with its LEAF. In seven years, Nissan tripled the range of its LEAF without making any radical technical breakthroughs. When Nissan launched the LEAF in 2011, it had a 24 kWh lithium-ion battery that gave it an EPA-rated range of 73 miles for a base price of $33,730, not including any tax credits. With little rise in the price, the range has steadily increased, first to 84 miles in 2013, and then to 107 miles with a 30 kWh battery in 2016.

In 2017, Nissan launched the second-generation LEAF with a 151-mile range and a 40 kWh battery. In 2019, for a premium of about $4,000, Nissan started offering the LEAF Plus with a range of 226 miles and a 62 kWh battery. The range increases were a result of incremental changes, including tweaks in battery chemistry, changes to the heating system, improvements in regenerative braking, reduction of body weight, and reduction of aerodynamic drag.

With a range of 226 miles, the LEAF Plus is close to the one-tank range of many gasoline-powered cars. While gasoline-powered car ranges are not increasing year to year, EV ranges are continuing to improve.

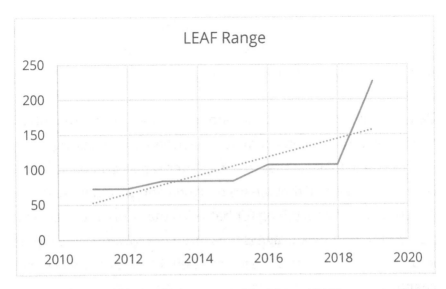

## LEAF Range

Look at how quickly the driving range of the Nissan LEAF has grown since 2011. The solid line shows the LEAF's actual EPA-tested range, and the dotted line shows the ten-year trend.

In a survey of potential buyers, Volvo found that 58 percent of respondents cited range as the biggest barrier to purchasing an EV. Driving habits of most Americans should make range a non-issue. According to the Bureau of Transportation Statistics, the average American drives twenty-nine miles per day, well within the range of all EVs. Despite this fact, consumers were uncomfortable with the short range of the original LEAF. They wanted a comfortable buffer for unanticipated errands. To alleviate most consumers' worries about not having enough range to get through their typical day or go on a trip, the comfort zone seems to be at or above two hundred miles per charge. Many new EVs on the market exceed this, and a three-hundred-plus mile range is becoming more and more common.

Range depends on several factors such as vehicle weight, rolling resistance of the tires, aerodynamics, whether heating and air conditioning are used, and driving style (rabbit starts versus chill driving). However, the biggest factor by far is how much energy the battery can store.

Batteries are the heaviest components in an EV, so manufacturers have made considerable investments in reducing their weight. The conflict is that to get greater range, you need more battery storage, and that means more weight. So, manufacturers are continuously searching for batteries that store more energy per weight. Battery storage is measured in kilowatt-hours (kWh) and is explained in the "Technical Definitions and Explainers" chapter.

The amount of energy stored in a battery divided by its weight is called the specific energy of the battery. Over the last twenty years, we've seen a steady improvement in EV-battery specific energy. They can provide more energy for less weight than ever before.

To get higher specific energy, the EV industry has changed battery types, tweaked the chemistry of specific battery types, and improved power-management electronics. All contribute to reducing weight and increasing range.

## CONNECTIVITY

We cannot overlook the importance of the connected car to the EV revolution. The recent success of EVs is due, in part, to a confluence of several technologies reaching maturity simultaneously. These include battery technology, low-cost computing power, and, interestingly, cellular technology.

Unlike gasoline-powered cars, EVs rely on cellular connectivity to update their sophisticated electronics and navigation systems. EVs have complex electronics for functions like power management and motor control. These systems are new and have a need for frequent software updates as improvements are developed.

It is much more important to update the navigation system in an EV than in a gasoline-powered vehicle. Although there are 168,000 gas stations in the US, the number of public electric-recharge stations is a fraction of this. In 2011, there were 3,394 public EV charging stations in the United States. By 2018, that number had grown to 61,067. As new charge stations are installed, their locations need to be pushed to EV navigation systems so that you can find that new charge station when you need it.

Finding new stations wouldn't be possible without the ability to update a car's navigation system via the cellular network. Like other costs of EV ownership, the cost of cellular connection has dropped. Over a ten-year period, the cost to connect wirelessly to vehicles dropped from dollars a month to pennies a month. This has made it possible for car manufacturers to continue to make updates after shipment to consumers.

## THE IMPORTANCE OF DESIGN

Great product design generates consumer desire. Yes, practicality and environmental concerns are important, but if the product doesn't arouse design desire, people are likely to pass.

Consumers have to connect with products in the market-place. Remember the crazy big fins on cars back in the 1960s. They served no purpose other than to build purchase desire.

Before the iPod, there were many unsuccessful MP3 players. Instead of being one of many MP3 players in the market, the iPod became an object of desire. This was as much due to the iTunes music library as it was due to the device's beautiful design. It was sleek with a cool user interface.

Just like the less-sexy MP3 players, EV models developed in the 1970s didn't build desire. They were utilitarian (although short on range), but their design didn't catch the public's eye. Design, for them, was an afterthought.

Look at the CitiCar made by Sebring-Vanguard, Inc. It may have been a good car, but would you want it parked in your driveway?

Making a good car with good driving range isn't enough. Tesla recognized this and has rocked the marketplace with designs consumers desire.

The Sebring-Vanguard CitiCar

In August of 2006, Elon Musk made a tongue-in-cheek post on the Tesla blog entitled, "The Secret Tesla Motors Master Plan," in which he stated that "the Tesla Roadster is designed to beat a gasoline sports car like a Porsche or Ferrari in a head-to-head showdown." He introduced a bit of machismo into the comparison between EV and gasoline-engine cars.

In April of 2009, Franz von Holzhausen, Tesla's chief designer, got more specific on the blog with a post about the Model S. The goal, he said, was "a mid-sized sedan that seats seven people and their luggage in a package that is both functional and good looking—actually, better looking than anything on the market." Tesla understood the critical importance of design, and the rest of the market followed.

2011 Tesla Model S

Tesla launched the Roadster in 2008. In 2011, Nissan followed by launching the LEAF. Nissan recognized the importance of educating the public about all electric vehicles, so it embarked on a twenty-two-city Zero Emission Tour of the United States. LEAF's debut was one of the best-coordinated launch events in history, with a three-tent "Epcot-like" event in each city. In 2012, Tesla launched the beautifully designed Model S.

2008 Tesla Roadster

2011 Nissan LEAF

The Model S went on to win the very prestigious *Motor Trend* Car of the Year. Not only did it win, but *Motor Trend* named the Model S sedan the best of all the cars that have won the publication's Car of the Year award in the last seventy years.

The latest major influencer is the Jaguar I-PACE. This is an up-market EV with a range of 234 miles. It has two drive motors and all-wheel-drive control, and it looks great. After launching in October 2018, it received a variety of impressive accolades including the European Car of the Year award. It is the only Jaguar to win this award. It also won the 2019 World Car of the Year. Yes, EVs are having a moment.

2018 Jaguar I-PACE

EV manufacturers are now adding good looks to great vehicles. The combination is sure to drive sales in 2021.

# FROM BIRTH THROUGH MATURATION – A HISTORY OF ELECTRIC VEHICLES

Before the first electric vehicle, the electric motor had to be invented. Famous scientist Michael Faraday built the world's first electric motor in 1821. This innovation resulted from his prior discovery that a magnetic field can generate an electric current. The race to electric power was on.

### Under the Hood

*Michael Faraday is one of the most important scientists of all time. His discoveries in chemistry, the physics of light, electricity, and magnetism changed the world. Einstein kept a picture of Faraday on his wall.*

*Three years after showing the world how an electric motor could work, Faraday invented the rubber balloon. Birthday parties, like all of science, were changed.*

As we tell you this short history of the electric vehicle (EV), please note the incredible fact that electric cars preceded gasoline and diesel cars. Electrics were far more advanced than internal-combustion vehicles. Forty years passed from the creation of the first electric car to the first gasoline-powered car. As we look back at the dawn of motorized vehicles, the logical question to ask is, what changed the favored technology from electric powered to oil powered?

The first six recorded land-speed records were all held by EVs. The land-speed record is defined as the highest speed achieved by a person using a vehicle on land. An EV was the first vehicle of any kind to drive faster than one hundred kilometers per hour (62 mph), and EVs have been driven on the moon during NASA Apollo missions 15, 16, and 17.

### Under the Hood

*We think electric cars are out of this world. History supports our contention. The only vehicles to drive on the moon have been EVs. A new electric car was developed and used in lunar exploration for each of NASA's Apollo missions from 15 to 17. NASA might sell one of these to you, but you would have to go get it.*

Almost immediately after the invention of the electric motor, the first electric carriage was built. Historians can argue who was first, but the choices seem to be either Robert Anderson, from Scotland, or American Thomas Davenport. Both built vehicles powered by electric batteries. There were many other inventors, especially in Europe, who advanced the field. But like most new technology, there were many false starts and partial successes.

Belgian electric vehicle called the La Jamais Contente is the first vehicle of any type in history to go over one hundred kilometers per hour (62 mph). 1899

Scotsman Robert Anderson built a crude electric carriage. Circa 1835

These early vehicles used car batteries that were very different from what we know today. They were one-time-use batteries that relied on chemical reactions that could not be reversed. Drivers couldn't recharge the battery; they had to use a new one.

The early cars worked, but, clearly, the chief obstacle to advancement was the battery. A major step forward was contributed by French physicist Gaston Planté, who, in 1859, invented the rechargeable lead-acid battery.

Gustave Trouve rode a three-wheeled electric vehicle in Paris in 1881. He made improvements to a purchased electric motor and used a newly developed rechargeable battery. Trouve kept innovating and used his electric motor and battery to power a boat on the river Seine easily beating gasoline-powered outboard engines.

Gustave Trouve riding in his three-wheeled electric car. 1881

The earliest model that we would recognize as an electric car was built by German engineer Andreas Flocken in 1888. European interest in electric vehicles was years ahead of American interest.

German inventor Andreas Flocken in 1888

In the middle of the nineteenth century, just like today, as new technologies were developed, creative people raced to improve the electric car. They were trying to eke out more miles per charge and more speed. In 1899, a Belgian electric vehicle called the La Jamais Contente became the first vehicle of any type to exceed a speed of one hundred kilometers per hour (62 mph). It was driven by two thirty-three-horsepower (25 kilowatt) electric motors powered by two eighty-cell lead-acid batteries manufactured by Fulmen from France.

## Under the Hood

*The first electric cars used direct-current motors. Today, the motors in EVs run on alternating current (AC). The man who invented the AC motor was Nikola Tesla.*

*Several inventors built AC motors before and at the same time Tesla did, but he was awarded a US patent for his invention in 1888.*

In our modern age, sixty-two miles per hour doesn't sound impressive. Consider a time before people had ever traveled so fast. There were questions as to whether people could think and function while traveling at such a speed. Electric cars and trains were the space frontier of the nineteenth century.

The first practical electric vehicle in the United States is believed to have been developed by William Morrison of Des Moines, Iowa, in 1890. Morrison was a chemist, and his first contribution was improving the battery system to power the motors. With an improved power source, he built a six-passenger vehicle capable of going 14 mph. Not an astonishing speed, but faster than a horse-drawn carriage could go.

Morrison's invention marked the start of the first golden age of electric vehicles. From the late 1890s to the early 1900s, there was a steady interest in electric vehicles. Unlike their early gas-powered competitors, electric vehicles did not require pump priming and hand cranking to start, had no smelly gasoline, and were essentially maintenance-free. This made EVs more attractive than early internal-combustion engines, which were temperamental and difficult to start and operate.

Founded in 1899 in Cleveland, Ohio, the Baker Motor Vehicle Company was one of the most successful manufacturers in the first golden age of EVs. The first Baker Electric model was the two-seater Imperial Runabout. Thomas Edison bought one as his first car. By 1905, Baker's annual production was approximately four hundred cars, which was reportedly three times as many cars as any other EV manufacturer at the time.

Baker Motor Vehicle Company from Cleveland, OH, launches its first vehicle, the two-seater Imperial Runabout. 1902

In 1909, Emil Gruenfeldt, an engineer with Baker Motor Vehicle Company, drove his Baker Electric Roadster 160.8 miles (259 km) on a single charge. This would have been impressive in 2009, let alone 1909. The 1912 Baker Electric Victoria was used by five First Ladies of the United States.

As more American homes got electric service, more people purchased electric vehicles. However, three competing technologies were racing for dominance. At the turn of the twentieth century, 40 percent of cars were powered by steam. Electrics held a 38 percent market share, and internal-combustion vehicles held the lowest share, at 22 percent. With rich interiors, electrics were expensive and appealed to the wealthy. Enter the Model A, made as inexpensively as possible. This led the market share of electrics to fall.

Henry Ford changed the factory manufacturing system forever and made thousands of gasoline-powered vehicles at rock-bottom prices. His vision was that everyone should drive a Ford. He kept prices down so low that he only made a miserly profit on each car.

Early EV adoption was further hindered by a lack of electric-power infrastructure. Electric utilities were reluctant to provide charging stations. At the same time, discoveries of petroleum reserves made gasoline affordable and widely available. Oil companies were delighted to build gas stations to sell their products. For about the next fifty years, internal-combustion-engine (ICE) technology developed rapidly while EV development stagnated.

This first golden age of EVs ebbed about the time that the US entered World War I. More refined and reliable gasoline-powered vehicles increased in popularity and gained infrastructural support. Early electric vehicles could not compete with the power-to-weight ratio afforded by internal-combustion systems.

EVs enjoyed a mild resurgence during the 1970s energy crisis. However, the EVs developed then were strictly utilitarian and failed to capture mass-market appeal. The oil shortage also launched small companies that converted existing manufactured gas vehicles into electric.

The California Air Resources Board (CARB) played a leading role in starting the new golden age of EVs. Although not specifying electric vehicles, they adopted a Zero Emission Vehicle (ZEV) mandate. The initial mandate ran from 1990 to 2003 and required that 2 percent of the vehicles manufactured for sale in

California by large automakers be zero-emission vehicles. The requirement rose to 5 percent in 2001 and 10 percent in 2003. California is the largest car market in the US, and manufacturers are forced to follow the mandates that CARB creates.

To meet the CARB mandate, large automakers developed electric vehicles. The Ford Ranger EV pickup truck and the Toyota RAV4 EV1 caught consumer attention.

Toyota launched the RAV4 EV in 1991

The fossil-fuel industry did not sit idly and watch this happening. They joined some large automakers to lobby against the mandate. They instigated a lawsuit that resulted in an injunction prohibiting CARB from enforcing the mandate.

CARB adopted amendments and redesigned the ZEV program to apply to model years 2015 and beyond. This ultimately relieved the pressure on large automakers to make EVs available to the wider market. Although the mass adoption of EVs was delayed, it was not stymied.

The problem for all car manufacturers was that battery technology wasn't good enough. To provide adequate driving range, hybrids were invented. These cars have both a gasoline engine and an electric motor. Since gasoline has a higher energy density, it can provide energy for longer rides by converting that chemical energy into electric energy that drives the car.

## Under the Hood

*Energy density is the amount of energy that can be stored in a volume of space. A gallon of gasoline has about one hundred times the energy of a lithium-ion battery of the same size. However, due to the inefficiency of internal-combustion engines, less than a third of the energy in a gallon of gas is utilized.*

Toyota first offered their hybrid model, Prius, in the late 1990s. It caught on partly due to its high gas mileage—forty to fifty miles per gallon—and partly due to its low tailpipe emissions. The Prius is owned by millions of people around the world.

Other car manufacturers were not convinced that hybrids were the way to go. Several invested in research on hydrogen fuel cells and batteries. Improvements in the technology of batteries, motors, and electronics all advanced enough to improve their market viability. Companies were developing cars tentatively.

GM introduced the modern-looking EV1 but didn't make it available for sale. Instead, consumers had to enter into a closed-end lease, meaning that the cars had to be returned to GM at the end of the lease. GM produced 1,117 EV1 cars. Unhappy with their own car, GM took back the cars at the end of their lease and destroyed them. For enthusiasts, this was crazy. This action heaped negative publicity on GM. Even if GM wasn't sold on EVs, there was enthusiasm among niche groups.

General Motors EV1 1996

The success and subsequent demise of the EV1 pushed Martin Eberhard to cofound Tesla, Inc. and produce the Roadster. The name *Tesla* comes from the Serbian inventor Nikola Tesla. Launched in 2008, the Tesla Roadster was embraced by early adopters. The car proved EVs are viable and, in some ways, more capable than ICE vehicles.

The Tesla Roadster 2008

Today we associate the name Elon Musk with Tesla Motors, but he didn't organize the company. Fresh off his success in selling his 11 percent share of PayPal, he invested in Tesla. Soon he became CEO and chairman of the board. Tesla builds more than electric cars. It also has a large manufacturing facility focused on batteries and owns a large company that makes solar panels.

Starting in 2012, sales of Tesla cars have accelerated as fast as its cars do. Today its total sales are just under one million units.

### Under the Hood

*Thomas Edison brought Nikola Tesla to America to work at Edison Machine Works. Tesla, a diligent worker and brilliant engineer, quit after a few months to start his own business. He made improvements to direct-current motors and developed much of the early equipment for alternating-current systems. While Edison strongly pushed for direct current, Tesla, and later George Westinghouse, fought for alternating current in what became the great war of currents. Among Tesla's many inventions was the first radio-controlled device. The device allowed Tesla to control the motor of a model boat.*

While Tesla was growing quickly, Nissan jumped into the electric car field as well. It launched the LEAF in 2010. It was the best-selling mass-market EV until it was recently eclipsed by Tesla models. In 2013, BMW launched the i3, followed by the Jaguar I-PACE in 2018. The year 2021 promises an EV explosion, with no fewer than twenty-five BEVs (battery electric vehicles) being offered to the US market.

The BMW i3 came to market in 2013

# EV ADVANTAGES

For years, pundits, mainly from the fossil-fuel industry, have promoted the idea that electric vehicles are worse for the environment than diesel or gasoline-powered vehicles because EVs are powered by dirty electricity. By *dirty*, they mean coal-fired power plants and the like. This assertion is completely wrong for many reasons.

---

### Under the Hood

*Gasoline-powered vehicles use more electricity than EVs. Say that with a loud voice at your next party and see what happens.*

---

Let's start with an amazing and wildly underreported fact. In addition to the fuel that they burn, gasoline-powered vehicles use more electricity than EVs. Yes, you read that correctly. Gas vehicles use more electricity than electric vehicles. How can this be? Let's run through the facts.

Pump jacks in Lost Hills Oil Field, Central California. It requires electricity to pump crude oil from the ground, distribute it and refine it into gasoline and diesel fuel. Pump jacks are used to extract crude oil. Most are powered by electric motors.

Producing gasoline or diesel fuel is an energy-intensive process. A conservative estimate is that it takes at least 8 kWh of electricity to drill, transport, and refine a gallon of gasoline. According to the U.S. Department of Energy, approximately 66% of domestic petroleum transport (by ton-mile) occurs by pipeline. Pipeline pumps are typically driven by electric motors.

According to the Environmental Protection Agency (EPA), the average American car can drive 25.1 miles on a gallon of gas. That means the average gas-powered vehicle consumes 31.8 kWh of electricity to travel 100 miles (in addition to emitting greenhouse gases from burning the gasoline).

Compare the electric power used by a standard-range Tesla Model 3. The Tesla Model 3 can cover one hundred miles without burning a drop of gasoline and while using only 21 kWh of electric power. So, the Tesla uses less electric power than the standard gasoline-powered car does to cover one hundred miles.

Wait, there's more. According to the EPA, a typical passenger vehicle emits about 4.6 metric tons of carbon dioxide per year while driving almost eleven thousand miles. This means that in addition to consuming more electricity than an EV, the typical gasoline-powered vehicle is emitting tons of noxious greenhouse gases.

This trend of improving technology will continue to accelerate in favor of EVs for a number of factors. One is that the electric grid is increasingly becoming greener as we generate more power from renewables and less from coal.

## PERFORMANCE

EV owners report that one of the most enjoyable features of driving their cars is the instant acceleration. Step on the accelerator and you are moving.

The faster acceleration is delivered by the torque that electric motors can deliver at low speeds. This is a significant advantage over gas-powered cars.

Torque is the rotational force that causes a shaft to spin. EVs' electric motors deliver 100 percent of their available torque instantaneously. They don't have to build up speed before they reach peak power. This enables them fast stoplight starts and superior passing ability.

An internal-combustion engine's power comes from a simple chemical reaction between fuel and oxygen. If you want more power, you must give it more fuel—hence the term "stepping on the gas." However, this isn't a quick process.

The fuel needs to flow through pipes into an intake manifold and then finally into the combustion chambers. The engine's hundreds of parts each have momentum that causes a lag when trying to get them to spin faster.

The biggest disadvantage that gas engines have with respect to torque output is their *power band*. The power band is the range of revolutions per minute (RPM) around peak power output. Electric motors usually have a flat power band, meaning that they deliver maximum torque the moment they start turning. Internal-combustion engines are different. They must reach a high enough speed before they reach their power band.

Even if an internal-combustion engine is capable of producing more power than an electric motor, it takes time to gain the RPM speed to hit its peak power. This is why EVs tend to accelerate much faster than ICE vehicles. The graphic below shows a rough comparison of an electric motor's torque output versus a gas engine. At some point, the power output of the electric motor will start to decline, but this will be after the car is going fast.

ICE vehicles have an additional disadvantage when it comes to acceleration. The internal-combustion engine needs to stay within its power band in order to maintain peak power output. It cannot go too fast or too slow (too many or too few RPM). To keep the engine within its optimal power band, ICE vehicles have a transmission with a clutch.

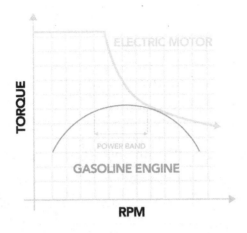

Graphs showing a rough comparison of the torque output from an electric motor versus an internal-combustion engine.

The transmission allows the wheels to turn fast or slow while keeping the engine within its optimal RPM range. Transmissions mesh different size gears to get different wheel speeds. A large gear connected to the motor will spin a small gear connected to the wheels very quickly. But to change from one gear to the next, the engine has to be disconnected momentarily from the drivetrain. The clutch is the device that does this.

When the clutch disengages the engine and drivetrain, the vehicle receives no power to the wheels. Pure EVs don't have clutches or transmissions and continue to power the wheels while the speed of the car changes.

### Under the Hood

*How many motors are in an EV? Most EVs are propelled by a single electric motor. Like internal-combustion cars, the motor drives either the front or rear wheels.*

*However, some EVs have a motor for the front wheels and a second motor for the rear wheels. This allows power to be shifted between the front and rear wheels to maintain stability in acceleration.*

*So, an EV can have either one or two motors. Some EVs, like variants of the Tesla Roadster or Cybertruck, have three motors. Two motors drive the two rear wheels individually, and one drives both front wheels.*

*To add to your confusion, some EVs, like the Rivian pickup truck and SUV, have one motor powering each wheel. So, the answer to the simple question is one, two, three, or four motors.*

## Efficiency

Compare EV and ICE technologies in terms of efficiency. Efficiency is the amount of energy that you put into a vehicle as gasoline or electricity compared to how much energy you get out to move you forward.

The US Department of Energy found that electric vehicles convert about 77 percent of received electrical energy from the grid to power at the wheels. Conventional gasoline vehicles only convert between 12 percent and 30 percent of the energy stored in gasoline to power at the wheels.

This makes EVs two to three times more efficient than gas-powered vehicles. So, even if electric cars are recharged with electricity generated by fossil-fuel-based sources, which is true in some cases, their motors are more efficient at transferring that energy stored in the batteries into motion. That means much less waste and a better deal for the environment.

Gasoline engines are riddled with inefficiencies. A significant portion of the energy from gasoline is converted to unwanted heat. Open the hood after driving even only a few miles, and you'll feel the heat. You'll feel the loss of energy. That's why gas-powered cars need complex and expensive radiator systems with their associated belts, pipes, and heat exchangers.

These amazing facts really shouldn't amaze us because we often see efficiency gains when we transition from one technology to another. For example, think about common household lighting over the last decade. Compact Fluorescent Lights (CFL) use about 70 percent less energy than incandescent bulbs, the oldest technology. LED lights, the newest technology, use about 50 percent less energy than comparable CFL bulbs. Equally impressive is that the average lifespan for a bulb has improved radically from incandescent to CFL to LED technology, moving from 1,200 hours to 8,000 hours to 25,000 hours, respectively.

## LITHIUM-ION BATTERIES

Two things you already know about lithium-ion batteries: they are rechargeable, and they use the element lithium. That is the important stuff to know. Here is the rest of the story.

Lithium is the lightest metal. A lithium ion is an atom of lithium that has a positive electric charge. The ion can form because it is easy to wrestle an electron, which carries a negative charge, away from the atom. A charged battery is loaded with lithium ions and an equal number of free electrons. These electrons can flow through a circuit as electricity to drive an EV.

When a lithium-ion battery is being used, ions move through the battery from the negative terminal towards the positive terminal. The free electrons can move by wire from the negative terminal to the motor and back to the positive terminal. The electrons recombine with the ions at the positive terminal to reconstitute lithium atoms.

When all the lithium ions have gained back an electron, the battery is discharged. It is time to reverse this process by charging the battery. As electrical energy is forced into the battery in charging, lithium atoms separate into ions and electrons. When no more lithium atoms can be broken down into ions and electrons, the battery is fully charged.

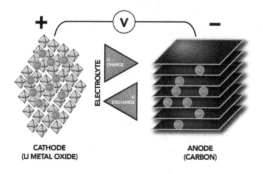

Lithium-ion battery

Why are lithium-ion batteries used in EVs? Lithium is a light material, and lithium-ion batteries are much lighter than traditional car batteries. They store much more energy per pound of weight than do the lead-acid batteries in an ICE vehicle.

Lithium-ion batteries are better at recharging than the previous generation, nickel-cadmium (nicad) batteries. Nicads have a memory effect. They won't recharge fully unless you discharge them fully. You couldn't top off your EV's tank to fill up the battery pack for a long drive tomorrow; you would have to drain the battery first and then refill it.

A Nobel Prize was awarded for the development of the lithium-ion battery.

## LOW COST OF OWNERSHIP

Even though the price of EVs has steadily declined and will continue to do so, they are still priced at a modest premium over their ICE counterparts. Some simple price comparisons can be made between the Hyundai Kona and the Hyundai Kona Electric or the MINI Cooper Hardtop two-door and the MINI Electric. However, when it comes to cost of ownership, the data is very clear. EVs are much cheaper to operate and maintain. We decided to compare costs over a five-year period.

---

### Under the Hood

*An ICE vehicle will cost about 4½ times more to operate and maintain than a comparable EV.*

---

Do you look at the price of gasoline every time you pull into a gas station? That's one of the larger costs of operating an ICE vehicle. If you drive as an average American does, you put about 10,500 miles on your odometer each year. Over five years, that is 52,500 miles. Taking a national average of 25.1 miles per gallon, that equates to 2,091 gallons of gasoline consumed over five years.

In February 2020, the national average price of gas was $2.44 for regular and $3.11 for premium. For this comparison, we use the price of regular. That means that the typical gasoline-powered car owner will pay about $5,100 for gas over five years.

Determining the cost to charge an EV is trickier than determining the straightforward gasoline-consumption cost. The majority of the time, EV owners charge their vehicles at home or at work. For our simple comparison, we assumed that drivers charge their cars at home instead of using a public charging station. To determine at-home charging costs, we took the average cost of electricity for the home in the United States in February 2020, which was $0.1282 per kilowatt (kW). The average EV will use 10,900 kW to drive the American average of 52,500 miles. That means that the typical EV owner will pay about $1,400 to charge their vehicle.

So, over a five-year period, the typical US EV driver saves $3,700 in the cost of fuel. The average EV driver also saves a ton of time and some aggravation by not having to go to gas stations.

Besides saving on fuel costs, EVs save money on brake maintenance. EVs save wear and tear on their brake pads and rotors by using the resistance of their motors to slow down and stop. This is called regenerative braking, and it drastically reduces the wear on the brakes.

EV owners can expect to get at least 150,000 miles from their brakes before they need servicing. On the other hand, gasoline-powered vehicles do not have regenerative braking. According to Kelley Blue Book (KBB), the average lifespan for brake pads on a gasoline-powered vehicle is about 40,000 miles. KBB states that the average cost to replace pads ranges between $150 and $300 per axle. We chose a midpoint of $225 per axle. That means on average, ICE-car drivers pay $450 every 40,000 miles to have all four brakes (two on each axle) serviced.

A third cost of operating a gasoline- or diesel-powered car is changing oil. The electric motors in EVs do not require oil. AAA used to recommend changing oil every 3,000 miles. Newer synthetic lubricants extend this range to between 5,000 and 7,500 miles.

For cost comparisons, we use an oil-change window of 7,500 miles. Thus, over our five-year operating-cost comparison between EVs and ICEs, the ICE owner would change oil seven times. KBB estimates that oil changes cost between $65 and $125. We use a midpoint cost of $95, which suggests a cost of $665 to change the oil seven times.

Here is a table summarizing the costs of fuel and maintenance over a five-year period. Obviously, we are leaving out many potential repair bills that are impossible to predict. Of the maintenance items we know about, it is clear that electric vehicles are much less expensive to operate. We estimate the savings at $4,815.

| Cost to Operate and Maintain Over Five Years | | |
|---|---|---|
| | EV | ICE |
| "Fuel" | $1,400 to charge | $5,100 for gas |
| Brakes | $0 | $450 |
| Oil | $0 | $665 |
| Total | $1,400 | $6,215 |

Because electric-motor drive systems have so many fewer parts, they experience far fewer repairs. Here is a list of the most common gas-vehicle repairs that you will never have to worry about if you own an EV.

- replacing an oxygen sensor
- replacing a catalytic converter
- replacing ignition coil(s) and spark plug(s)
- tightening or replacing a fuel cap
- thermostat replacement
- replacing ignition coil(s)
- mass airflow sensor replacement
- replacing spark plug wire(s) and spark plug(s)
- replacing evaporative-emissions (EVAP) purge-control valve
- replacing evaporate-emissions (EVAP) purging solenoid

If over the last five years, your car required any of these repairs, you know how expensive they are. The bottom line is that a gasoline-powered vehicle will cost about 4½ times more to operate and maintain than a comparable EV.

## RELIABILITY

Due to their engineering simplicity, EVs are far more reliable than gasoline-powered vehicles. It is difficult to get an exact parts count, but it is clear that EVs have fewer moving parts in their drivetrains than cars with internal-combustion engines. More parts, and especially more moving parts, mean more potential points of failure.

According to Tesla, their drivetrain only has about seventeen moving parts compared to the two thousand or so in a typical drivetrain of an ICE vehicle. Internal-combustion engines have pistons, valves, camshafts, and oil pumps whirling around at high speeds. None of these exist in an EV. Furthermore, most EVs do not change gears, so there is no need for a complex and expensive transmission and clutch that needs to be maintained.

When Nissan started selling the first mass-produced EV on the market in 2011, there were concerns about the LEAF's batteries degrading over time. Now that we have almost ten years of data, we know that this isn't a concern.

Data generated from a large sample size of European Tesla Model S and Model X owners provides more evidence. After driving approximately 168,000 miles, the batteries still had

91 percent of their original capacity. The data shows that the batteries lose about 1 percent of capacity every 18,750 miles.

The electric motor in an EV can deliver solid performance for more than fifteen years. There are several factors that determine how long it lasts. Fluctuations in the charging voltage can decrease its life, as can excessive environmental heat. Some experts predict that, under normal driving conditions, the motor can last twenty years—much longer than the car itself.

Consumer Reports estimates that EV batteries should last two hundred thousand miles. That's fifteen to twenty years of driving before the batteries need to be replaced. At that point, the batteries wouldn't go to a landfill; they would probably be used as a home battery bank to store solar- and wind-generated electric power during the day and provide it to the household at night.

Car manufacturers are providing warranties on batteries up to one hundred thousand miles. Check the warranty on any car you are considering purchasing. Of course, the numbers we present here may vary from manufacturer to manufacturer.

## What Is Regenerative Braking?

When you need to slow down to off-ramp speed while cruising along at sixty miles per hour, your car needs to reduce its energy of motion. In internal-combustion-engine vehicles or on your bicycle, you apply the brakes, which decreases kinetic energy (the energy of motion), transforming it into heat. Touching the brakes after driving will convince you that heat has been generated. Be careful not to burn yourself.

The heat that results from braking is lost to the environment. The brakes cool by sharing their heat with the air. Of course, you paid for that energy at the gas pump, and in using the brakes, you are tossing that energy away.

The energy doesn't go away, but it is no longer available to you as a resource. The energy changes to a form, heat, that doesn't benefit you.

In an EV, a process called regenerative braking captures some of that energy instead of transforming it into heat through the brakes. Regenerative braking does this by operating the electric-drive motor in reverse.

We normally think of electric motors as converting electric energy into kinetic energy. They take electricity and produce motion. Electric motors are just as happy to work in reverse. They can take kinetic energy and make electric energy. Aside from solar voltaic cells, this is how almost all electricity is generated.

To generate the electricity you use at home, a large force is needed: water behind a dam, wind blowing through huge turbine blades, or steam turning turbine blades in a nuclear reactor or fossil fuel power plant. The captured motion turns a giant motor, and the motor converts the spinning motion into electricity. Motors running in reverse are called generators.

An electric car uses the energy of motion or the energy of position (for instance, sitting atop a hill), to generate electricity. This not only recaptures some of the energy that went into accelerating the car or powering it up a hill, it also reduces the need for brakes. Although some drivers occasionally downshift to slow their vehicle, an internal-combustion engine cannot do this as efficiently or conveniently.

So how much energy can regenerative braking save? It turns out quite a bit. Each car model is different, and a typical range is 60–70 percent of the energy that otherwise would be lost. The bigger and heavier the vehicle, the bigger the savings are.

This savings only pertains to the energy lost during braking. You only get the 70 percent savings when you are braking or going down a hill.

Energy savings plays out very favorably in extending the range of an EV. Reports show that range extension can be as little as 15 percent or as high as 30 percent. The more stop-and-go driving you do or the more long hills in your route, the more your energy savings are boosted. Regenerative braking also reduces wear on the vehicle's brake pads and rotors. This saves the owner money by reducing how often the brakes need to be serviced.

## One-Pedal Driving

Regenerative braking slows the car down as soon as you lift your foot off the accelerator. This can cause a rapid slowing or a gradual slowing depending on the car manufacturer. A test drive will let you get the feel for how quickly the car slows.

Some manufacturers allow you to change how quickly the car slows; throw a switch or make an adjustment on the touch screen to increase or decrease the rate of slowing.

Of course, there is also a brake pedal. If you need a sudden stop, you press it, just as you would in an internal-combustion-engine vehicle. This pedal is also needed in order for the car to come to a complete stop. Regenerative braking slows the car, but won't keep it at a stop when sitting at a red light.

Regenerative braking has minimal impact on range during highway driving because you don't brake often. However, it can significantly improve range when driving in stop-and-go city traffic.

# EV MYTHS

Why do we have a chapter on EV myths, and where do these myths come from? There is a lot of misinformation about EVs. Some of it is old information that persists, and some is deliberately sowed to discourage people from purchasing EVs.

EVs will herald a revolution in transportation, creating winners and losers. The industries that will lose market share and revenue want to slow this revolution or totally derail it. These industries include energy companies as well as manufacturers and retail sales groups that sell ICE cars. According to the *Washington Post*, one fossil-fuel interest group has committed spending up to $10 million per year to spread misinformation about electric vehicles and bolster a positive public opinion of fossil-fuel usage.

EVs will not provide the service revenue and profits for car dealers that ICE vehicles do. With EVs, there are no oil changes, spark-plug changes, emissions-systems inspections, or timing-belt changes. Brake maintenance will be much less frequent.

This is a great deal for EV owners. However, since so much of a dealer's profit comes from service, and as EVs will greatly reduce the need for service, traditional dealers aren't thrilled with the revolution.

Of course, there is also a lot of information out there that may have been true three or five years ago but is now out of date. The developments in technology, especially those related to batteries and car-computer systems, have been mind-bendingly rapid. Reading any publication or data source that is more than a year or so old could give you false impressions of what is happening with EVs.

## Myth 1: EVs Do Not Have Enough Range to Be Viable

Reality: Ten years ago, this was no myth. For example, in 2011, the Nissan LEAF was the first mass-market EV, and it had an effective range of 75 miles. The LEAF now has a range of 226 miles.

The average range of the twenty-two mass-market EVs shipping in North America in 2021 is 284 miles. The average range of a gasoline-powered car is about 275 miles. The myth of limited range is debunked.

## Myth 2: EVs Are Not Safe to Drive

EVs are actually safer than gas-powered vehicles for two reasons. First, due to their typical battery placement, EVs tend to have lower centers of gravity than gas-powered cars.

Having a low center of gravity makes an EV less likely to roll over. This is important because, according to the US Department of Transportation, rollovers have a higher fatality rate than other kinds of crashes. With more weight below you in an EV, you are safer.

Second, a common cause of injury during a head-on collision is the internal-combustion engine being pushed backward into the passenger compartment. The large block of metal has nowhere to go except into your lap.

An EV motor is much smaller and lighter than a gas or diesel engine. This has a few benefits. First, there is less heavy metal to be pushed back into the passenger compartment, causing injury. Second, EV motors are so small that they leave room for the manufacturers to put a trunk, or "frunk," in the front of the car.

Where did the engine go? Under the Hood of an EV, there is enough room for a trunk.

What is all this stuff? An ICE vehicle's engine compartment is stuffed full of heavy metal.

Also, with the smaller electric motor, there is more empty space under the hood. When a crash occurs, that "crumple zone" will absorb much of the impact. The crumple zone acts like a shock absorber.

The United States National Highway Traffic Study tests car models to assess how safe they are. In their forty-nine-year history of testing cars, the Tesla Model 3 is the safest. The Model 3, an EV, has the lowest probability of injury in a crash of any car.

Maybe the Model 3 stands alone in safety among EVs. So what were the second and third safest cars in the study? The Tesla Model S and the Tesla Model X. Tesla swept the top three rankings. Myth busted.

## Myth 3: EVs Are Not Greener than Gasoline or Diesel-Powered Cars

Sometimes you can see a totally bogus claim with your eyes. Stopped at any intersection, you can see plumes of exhaust arising from ICE cars, especially those that need a tune-up. From the tailpipe of an EV, what do you see? You can't even see the tailpipe, let alone exhaust, because there isn't any.

Those exhaust plumes from ICE cars are composed of several greenhouse gases that we don't want to add to the atmosphere. Getting the gasoline from the ground into the tank of an ICE car uses more electricity than an EV uses in driving. That is, a gasoline-engine car that is sitting still has used more electricity than an EV will use to drive.

Clearly not an electric vehicle

Exploring for oil, pumping it out of the ground, shipping it, and refining it into gasoline and diesel is an energy-intensive process. EVs will continue to get greener as the power grid gets greener. ICE vehicles will remain dirty.

According to the US Energy Information Association, US renewable electricity generation has doubled since 2008. Almost 90 percent of the increase in renewable energy came from wind- and solar-power generation. As of 2018, renewables provided 17.6 percent of electricity generation in the United States.

Meanwhile, internal-combustion engines are burning gasoline and diesel fuel and emitting into the atmosphere more than half of the total carbon monoxide and nitrogen oxides that humanity releases, and almost a quarter of the hydrocarbons.

## Myth 4: Electric Vehicles Are Slow

How fast do you need to go? Starting from a stop, EVs accelerate much faster than gas-powered vehicles. You might notice that drag racing today separates EVs from ICE vehicles because EVs usually win.

EVs accelerate faster because electric motors deliver 100 percent of their available power instantaneously. Unlike internal-combustion engines, EVs provide full torque at low RPM. Internal-combustion engines have to be spinning faster to deliver maximum torque or power. This enables EVs' fast launches and superior passing ability.

Not only do EVs accelerate faster, but their faster acceleration costs the consumer less. For example, the gas-powered Ford Mustang Mach-E GT costs $65,000 to deliver an acceleration from zero to sixty miles per hour in 3.5 seconds. That's fast, but for $10,000 less, the Tesla Model 3 Performance gets you up to speed in 3.2 seconds—even faster. For almost twice the price, at $99,000, a Porsche 911 is slower, at 4.0 seconds. Once you reach highway speeds, both ICE cars and EVs deliver power enough to move you down the road.

## Myth 5: EVs Are Expensive to Maintain

EVs are much less expensive to maintain. The three big costs of operating a gasoline-powered vehicle are gas, oil changes, and brake replacement.

The cost of fuel for an EV is much lower—about a quarter as expensive as an ICE vehicle covering the same driving distance. The low cost of electric energy and the high efficiency of electric motors make EVs much cheaper to "fuel" than gasoline-powered vehicles. What does gasoline cost you? Compare that to about $0.75 per equivalent distance driven by an EV.

EVs don't require oil changes. Isn't that nice—not having to take your car in every few thousand miles to change the oil? Perhaps you crawl under your car in the driveway with wrench in hand to do the job?

Because EV brakes last so much longer, they need to be replaced much less often. That saves a few hundred dollars. The brakes last longer because EVs use the motor to slow your forward motion, which takes some of the load off the brakes. This is called regenerative braking.

Because electric motors are far less complex than engines, the ten most common repairs performed on an ICE vehicle simply don't exist on an EV. This not only saves repair costs; it also saves the inconvenience of having your car in the shop instead of available to drive. The low cost of operation and maintenance for an EV are among its strongest selling points.

## Myth 6: There Aren't Enough Public Charging Stations

The number of EV charging stations in the United States is growing rapidly. The Department of Energy reports that the US now has over 20,000 EV charging stations, with more than 82,000 connectors. That's up from two years ago when there were about 16,000 public EV charging stations with about 43,000 connectors—an increase of 38 percent.

Tesla is one of the larger providers of charging stations. They have 1,971 Supercharger Stations with 17,467 connectors, most positioned along major highways. The other big players are ChargePoint, with 30,000 connectors, and Electrify America, with 12,000 charging stations and 35,000 connectors.

There is a tendency to compare public EV charge stations with gas stations. Most EV owners charge their cars at home, which is not an option for internal-combustion-engine vehicles. So, it is a bogus comparison to look at the number of gas stations versus the number of public charging stations when there are many thousands of residential charging stations.

## Myth 7: EV Batteries Don't Last and Will Cause a Recycling Problem

EVs on the market today use lithium-ion batteries. When Nissan started selling the first mass-produced EV in 2011, there were concerns about the LEAF's batteries degrading over time. With ten years of experience, we know that these batteries lose about 1 percent of capacity every 18,750 miles, or less than 20 percent after 200,000 miles. Of course, the results will vary from manufacturer to manufacturer, but the general trend holds. Another point of confidence is that electric vehicles are federally mandated to carry separate warranties for their battery packs for at least eight years or 100,000 miles.

Regarding recycling, gas-powered vehicles use lead-acid batteries. According to Battery Council International, lead-acid batteries have a recycling rate of 99.3 percent, making them the number one recycled consumer product in the US. Lithium-ion batteries are made from more valuable metals and rare-earth elements, making them more likely to be commercially recycled. It is also worth noting that EV batteries typically won't go from the vehicle to the recycling plant because they will still have useful capacity. Many used EV batteries will have a post-vehicle life storing solar energy or wind energy, or in other power-grid applications.

## Myth 8: EVs Are Too Expensive

When it comes to comparing the price of EVs to comparable gas-powered cars, it depends on the market segment. For example, in the luxury mid-size category, EVs are priced at or below the price of comparable gas-powered cars. Some examples are as follows.

| Luxury Mid-Size Category | | | |
|---|---|---|---|
| Gasoline-Powered | | Electric Vehicles | |
| Car | Starting MSRP | Car | Starting MSRP |
| BMW 330i | $41,250 | Ford Mach-E | $44,995 |
| Audi A4 | $44,600 | Tesla Model 3 | $37,990 |

In the economy market segment today, EVs are still priced at a premium, but you will need to factor in incentives. The US federal government and state governments offer tax credits, tax deductions, and other incentives that lower the cost of buying and operating an EV. The largest tax deduction is the $7,500 that is offered by the US federal government. This deduction no longer applies to Tesla because they have shipped too many electric vehicles to qualify for the program, but it does apply to other manufacturers.

When it comes to filling the "tank" and maintenance, EVs are much less expensive. As we outlined in our "Cost of Owner-ship" section, an ICE vehicle will cost about 4½ times more to operate and maintain than a comparable EV.

## Myth 9: The Electrical Grid Can't Support Millions of EVs

National Renewable Energy Lab research concludes that the existing grid can support current EV charging load and the demand that would occur if 25 percent of the cars on the road were electric. One reason is that a majority of EVs are charged when grid demand is low. It is also important to note that EVs won't reach 25 percent market share for some time. After that, grid-infrastructure upgrades can be made gradually and locally on a neighborhood-by-neighborhood basis. There won't suddenly be a need to upgrade the entire national grid infra-structure.

## Under the Hood

*The grid is the network of wires and transformers that deliver electricity from where it is produced to your home.*

# ELECTRIC VEHICLE TYPE CHOICES

This book focuses on battery electric vehicles (BEVs), which are often referred to as "pure EVs" because they do not use gasoline or diesel fuel in any way. However, there are other types of electrified vehicles which, in our opinion, were interim steps to finally achieving mass-market BEVs. Because the various types can be confusing, we decided to summarize them.

## Battery Electric Vehicles

Battery electric vehicles are 100 percent powered by rechargeable batteries. Their main components are batteries, one or more motors, and a motor control system that manages torque, traction slip, and regenerative braking. All vehicles in our Buyer's Guide are BEVs.

Cars designed as BEVs differ significantly from vehicles powered by internal-combustion engines. Vehicles need to be designed as BEVs to get all the advantages offered by a pure electric drivetrain. Some manufactures have converted existing gas-powered chassis to electric. A current example is the Kia Niro, which is available in either gas-powered or electric. Without making major modifications, they removed the internal-combustion engine, transmission, and other associated components and replaced them with batteries, an electric motor, and necessary EV electronics.

Because conversion vehicles were not designed specifically to be BEVs, they typically won't be able to fully leverage the features of a specifically designed BEV. For example, a vehicle specifically designed to be an EV will tend to have its batteries placed lower in the car, giving it a lower center of gravity. A lower center of gravity makes a car more stable and safer because it is less likely to roll over.

Specifically designed BEVs have a larger crumple zone in the front of the car. With many fewer parts in the engine compartment, there is more empty space. In a collision, the body of the car can crumple, which absorbs some of the energy of the crash. This reduces the likelihood or severity of injury during a collision.

## HYBRID ELECTRIC VEHICLES

Hybrid Electric Vehicles (HEVs) combine features of both EVs and ICE vehicles. They typically have one electric motor, one gasoline engine, and all the associated complexity and cost of each.

Since 1999, there have been over fifty hybrid vehicles offered in the United States. Some of the first were the Toyota Prius,

Toyota Camry Hybrid, and Ford Fusion Hybrid. HEVs started to gain popularity in 2005 and peaked around 2012. As battery technology has improved, BEVs' ranges have improved, and they have steadily taken market share from HEVs.

Hybrid vehicles have been a way for automakers to appease the automotive dealer groups on whom they depend for distribution and sales. Automotive dealers make about 80 percent of their profit from "the back of the shop"—providing vehicle service. Because EVs do not require oil changes, tune-ups, or frequent brake changes, some dealer groups have tried to delay the introduction of pure EVs. Hybrid vehicles have both internal-combustion engines and electric drivetrains, appeasing both the dealer groups that want the income from servicing vehicles and the public's demand for more fuel-efficient vehicles.

Using two power systems, one electric and one fossil fuel, gives car manufacturers lots of options for creative designs. There are five types of hybrids, and who knows if more types will be coming.

## PARALLEL HYBRID

Both the electric motor and the gasoline engine power the car. The tricky part comes in making a transmission that takes power from both.

You may be used to manual and automatic transmissions. A third type of transmission is becoming more common: continuously variable transmission (CVT). First used in sawmills in the late nineteenth century, it has found application in motorcycles and cars. It is the type of transmission used in snowmobiles.

CVTs don't use gears to transmit power from the engine and motor to the drive wheels. They use belts. The belts slide along conical-shaped pulleys that allow for different ratios of speed.

Both the motor and the engine are connected to one of the conical pulleys, as is the drivetrain. Either engine or motor can drive the car independently, or they can work together to do so.

Several manufacturers use CVT, including Toyota, Hyundai, Kia, Lexus, Ford, Nissan, Infiniti, Lincoln, and Honda.

## Series Hybrid or Range-Extended Electric Vehicles

Typically called range-extended hybrid electric vehicles (REHEV or REX), these are electric-motor-driven cars with a "spare tank." A gasoline engine consumes gasoline to generate electricity that replenishes the batteries that power the motor. The gas engine is not connected to the drivetrain.

The extended-range advantage of a hybrid is allowed by the energy density of gasoline. You can store a lot more energy in a cubic foot of gasoline than a cubic foot of electrical battery. Before today's more efficient batteries were available, having an engine was a way to extend the driving range without cramming the car full of batteries.

These hybrids provide an almost pure electric-powered ride with much less vibration than traditional gasoline or diesel-powered cars. It is a bit odd, though, for the gasoline engine to kick in and shut off at intervals that meet the needs of the battery and not the obvious up-and-down challenges of the road.

These vehicles are not pure electric and thus require fossil-fuel type maintenance on the motor, such as oil changes. However, REHEV do enable great gas mileage. Some models can be recharged via electrical outlets, but others cannot.

The Chevy Volt and the BMW i3 REX are examples of extended-range hybrids. With BEV prices falling and ranges increasing, the added cost and complexity of gasoline range extenders are difficult to justify.

## PLUG-IN HYBRID ELECTRIC VEHICLES

A plug-in hybrid electric vehicle (PHEV) is a hybrid electric vehicle with larger batteries that can, like an EV's, be plugged into an external power source. This gives PHEVs more electric range than a standard hybrid vehicle. Early PHEVs were the result of hobbyists installing aftermarket conversion kits into the trunks of their hybrid vehicles.

The Toyota Prius was the most popular target for plug-in upgrades. Originally the Prius had a plug-in conversion craze. This was short-lived, however, because the kits were relatively expensive and difficult to install. The conversion took up trunk space and could cause the vehicle's factory warranty to be voided.

Eventually, PHEVs were offered by vehicle manufacturers. A couple examples of PHEVs offered from manufactures were the Toyota Prius Plug-In Hybrid, the Honda Accord Plug-In Hybrid, and the Chevy Volt.

## HYBRIDS WITH LIGHTWEIGHT MOTORS

Instead of relying on a powerful electric motor to move the car with assistance provided by a gasoline engine, "mild hybrids" rely on a gasoline engine to do the bulk of the heavy lifting. This design uses an electric motor to assist the gasoline engine when it needs a boost.

Electric motors are great for accelerating from a complete stop, while gasoline engines are much slower. So mild hybrids use an electric motor at stoplights. The gasoline engine stops to save fuel, and the motor is ready to take off when you stomp on the accelerator.

The motor can assist in going up hills or elsewhere when the onboard computer decides it is needed. The mild hybrid saves fuel but doesn't give you zero tailpipe emissions or the less expensive fuel bill that a BEV does.

All of the previous hybrids are considered "full hybrids," which means that the electric motor is capable of moving the car by itself, even if it is for a short distance. In a mild hybrid, it cannot. Just as in a full hybrid, a mild hybrid's electric motor is there to assist the gasoline engine for the purposes of improving fuel economy, increasing performance, or both. It also serves as the starter for the automatic start-stop system, which shuts down the engine when the car comes to rest in order to save fuel.

Some car companies are using mild hybrid design. Dodge, Mercedes, and Audi are examples. It will be interesting to see if mild hybrids gain market acceptance or wither away as BEV technology continues to improve.

## OTHER HYBRIDS

Some manufacturers, like Honda, are making cars that aren't really series or parallel hybrids. In these vehicles, the engine spends most of its operating time generating electricity to charge the batteries, but the engine is able to assist the motor in propelling the car when needed.

Another variation is being made by Volvo. Their model uses a gasoline-powered engine for front-wheel drive (FWD) and an electric motor to drive the rear wheels. This arrangement is called "through-the-road hybrid." Switch the electric motor to the front and you have the same setup as performance models like the Porsche 918 Spyder and the BMW i8.

## FUEL-CELL ELECTRIC VEHICLES

Fuel-Cell Electric Vehicles (FCEVs), also referred to as hydrogen vehicles, use hydrogen as the main source of power. The hydrogen is fed into one side of a fuel cell. Oxygen, drawn from the surrounding air, enters the other side. The hydrogen is stripped of its electrons, and the oxygen is stripped of its protons. The resulting current charges the batteries.

Refueling an FCEV car with hydrogen at a hydrogen fuel station.

The combination of hydrogen and oxygen produces water, which drips to the ground. You might think that the trail of water would be noticeable, but it is not. FCEVs emit about the same amount of water that gasoline-powered cars do.

One more comparison between FCEVs and ICE vehicles. One gallon of gasoline will give a driving range of about twenty-five miles. One gallon of hydrogen will deliver sixty miles of range.

The energy conversion process in FCEVs is clean, but the end-to-end production process is inefficient and can be very dirty. Ninety-five percent of hydrogen is formed by steam heating or reforming natural gas. This process combines high-temperature steam with natural gas to extract hydrogen. Hydrogen production by steam reforming yields less energy than the natural gas at the beginning of the process. It also creates a lot of pollution. Since it uses natural gas, this is a non-green source of energy.

A small percentage of hydrogen is generated by electrolysis, using electricity to separate hydrogen and oxygen from water—a favorite demonstration in chemistry class. The conclusion of the demo is recombing the two gases in a window-shaking explosion. It requires more energy input than steam reforming and is only 70 percent efficient.

The "hydrogen economy" has been touted in some circles, especially in California during the early 1990s. There are many reasons why hydrogen hasn't caught on as a means of propulsion. The main reason is its relatively high cost due to its inefficiency. Let's make a quick comparison of FCEV operational cost to BEV.

The average rate per kilowatt was $0.1282 in the United States in February 2020. This means that it would cost about ten dollars to charge a large 75 kWh EV battery. An equivalent FCEV would require five kilograms of hydrogen, which would cost about $85—or more than eight times the cost to charge the EV.

The main problem with hydrogen is that it is expensive to produce because the processes are energy-intensive. Additional costs are the transportation and storage of hydrogen. Hydrogen gas has to be compressed or liquefied, which results in further loss of efficiency. All told, the end-to-end hydrogen process is about 50 percent less efficient than battery-powered vehicles.

Another big challenge with hydrogen as fuel is the lack of filling stations. An increase in filling stations won't occur until there are more FCEVs on the road, and there won't be more FECVs on the road until there are more filling stations.

Lastly, FCEVs are more complex than BEVs and require much more maintenance. Unless a major breakthrough occurs, it seems that FCEVs will be bypassed quickly by BEVs.

# EV BUYING GUIDE

As we mentioned earlier, most of today's EVs have overcome the main consumer objections of price, range, and styling. 2021 will be an exciting year, with far more EV options than ever before from which to choose.

Our 2021 guide is focused on the North American passenger car and truck mass market. To help you compare EVs, we laid out what we find to be the most useful specifications.

Our guide is not meant to duplicate the vast and varied information that you can find on the web. Rather, it is meant to act as a convenient, well-organized starting point for you to see what vehicles are available. We also provide you with insights about the various automakers and their design choices. We list these in alphabetical order by manufacturer and model name.

## Audi e-tron

Following the Tesla Model X and the Jaguar I-PACE, the Audi e-tron is the third luxury electric SUV to be launched. The Mercedes-Benz EQC will be the fourth when it launches in 2021.

The Audi e-tron is currently available as an SUV. It is bigger than Audi's Q5 but a little smaller than the Q8. Later in 2020, a second body type, called the SportBack, is expected to enter the North American market. It will have the same chassis, but a different body style.

True to form, Audi's e-tron provides the greatest passenger comfort. The cabin is trimmed in premium materials. The seats are nicely padded, with those in front being heated, cooled, and massage-capable. It has Audi's Virtual Cockpit with a head-up display. The ride is very quiet due to Audi's investment in sound insulation. The e-tron is a dual-motor, all-wheel-drive SUV. Roof rails come standard, and it can tow up to four thousand pounds.

| | |
|---|---|
| Starting Price (MSRP) | $74,800 |
| Range (miles) | 204–218 |
| Availability | Started Shipping 2018 |
| Units Sold in US | Fewer than 10,000 |
| Vehicle Class | Luxury SUV |
| NHTSA Safety Rating (5-star) | 5/5 |
| NCAP Safety Rating (5-star) | 5/5 |
| Zero to 60 mph (secs) | 6.8 – 5.7 |
| Horsepower | 402 |
| Battery (kWh) | 95 |
| Cargo Area (ft3) | 28.5 |
| Length (in) | 193 |
| Drive (FWD, RWD, AWD) | AWD |
| Weight (lbs) | 5,754 |
| Basic Warranty | 4-Year, 50,000 Miles |
| Battery Warranty | 8-Year, 100,000 Miles |

# BMW i3

The BMW i3 has been shipping for six years and is available as a pure battery EV or in an extended-range (REX) version with a small two-cylinder gasoline engine that powers a generator to recharge the batteries.

It is one of the most unique looking cars on the market. The body is made from carbon-fiber-reinforced plastic that is strong and lightweight, but expensive. This body material is typically used only in exotic supercars.

The i3 has small outside dimensions but is surprisingly large inside due to BMW's well-designed space utilization. The interior has the high-end materials and attention to detail to be expected in a BMW. One disappointment is its relatively short range for its premium price.

| | |
|---|---|
| Starting Price (MSRP) | $44,450 |
| Range (miles) | 153 |
| Availability | Started Shipping 2013 |
| Units Sold in US | Fewer than 50,000 |
| Vehicle Class | Subcompact Luxury |
| NHTSA Safety Rating (5-star) | Not Rated |
| NCAP Safety Rating (5-star) | 4/5 |
| Zero to 60 mph (secs) | 8.8 – 7.2 |
| Horsepower | 168 |
| Battery (kWh) | 42.2 |
| Cargo Area (ft3) | 15.1 |
| Length (in) | 158 |
| Drive (FWD, RWD, AWD) | RWD |
| Weight (lbs) | 2,635 |
| Basic Warranty | 4-Year, 50,000 Miles |
| Battery Warranty | 8-Year, 100,000 Miles |

# BMW i4

The BMW i4 is expected to start shipping in 2021. General announcements have been made, but details and photos are not yet available.

In July 2020, BMW announced that it had shut down its Munich factory for a month to prepare for production of the i4. The i4 will be marketed as a four-door coupe. It will be built on BMWs Cluster Architecture (CLAR) platform. This platform uses steel, aluminum, and optional carbon fiber. CLAR will support both rear-wheel-drive and all-wheel-drive configurations. The platform will also support ICE, plug-in hybrid, and BEV drivetrains. One drawback is that the i4 will not be specifically designed for an EV configuration, which probably means that there will be design tradeoffs and constraints.

The i4 will use BMW's Generation 5 batteries that support fast charging. For comparison, it takes the current i3 hatchback about seventeen minutes to add sixty-two minutes of charge. The i4 should be able to achieve the same charge in one-tenth the time.

BMW has made a commitment to electrified vehicles, both hybrids and BEVs. Its chief engineer, Klaus Fröhlich, stated that the company will launch twenty-five new electrified models by 2023, twelve of which will be full EVs.

| Starting Price (MSRP) | To Be Announced |
|---|---|
| Range (miles) | 300–320 |
| Availability | 2021 |
| Vehicle Class | Luxury Mid-Size Sedan |
| Zero to 60 mph (secs) | 4.0 |
| Horsepower | 530 |
| Battery (kWh) | 80 |
| Drive (FWD, RWD, AWD) | RWD & AWD |

## Chevrolet Bolt

The Chevrolet Bolt is a front-motor, five-door subcompact hatchback. For 2020, GM increased the Bolt's driving range from 238 miles to an impressive 259.

The Bolt is surprisingly large inside for a car that looks small from the outside. There is ample front and rear passenger space for four or five occupants and enough room in the rear cargo hold for five carry-on bags.

One disappointment is the low-rent interior look for a car at its price point. It has lots of exposed plastic, and power-adjustable seats are not available. The modern touchscreen and digital instrument cluster somewhat make up for the lackluster interior.

The Bolt's base model is the LT. Although the Premier model adds a variety of features, it doesn't seem to justify the $4,400 price increase. One option is to add the LT trim package for $555 and the Driver Comfort package for $495.

Similar vehicles to consider are the new Hyundai Kona EV and Kia Niro EV, which offer similar range at a lower price. Overall, the Bolt is a good EV and worth checking out.

| | |
|---|---|
| Starting Price (MSRP) | $37,495 |
| Range (miles) | 259 |
| Availability | Started Shipping 2017 |
| Units Sold in US | Fewer than 75,000 |
| Vehicle Class | Subcompact Hatchback |
| NHTSA Safety Rating (5-star) | 5/5 |
| NCAP Safety Rating (5-star) | - |
| Zero to 60 mph (secs) | 6.7 |
| Horsepower | 200 |
| Battery (kWh) | 60 |
| Cargo Area (ft3) | 16.9 |
| Length (in) | 164 |
| Drive (FWD, RWD, AWD) | FWD |
| Weight (lbs) | 3,563 |
| Basic Warranty | 3-Years, 36,000 Miles |
| Battery Warranty | 8-Year, 100,000 Miles |

## Ford Mustang Mach-E

In November 2019, Mustang history was made. For the first time in fifty-five years, Ford announced that it was expanding its Mustang family. The Mach-E is the first Ford to be designed specifically as an electric vehicle. It is a sign of Ford's commitment to electric that they leveraged their iconic Mustang brand. The *Mach-E* name is a tribute to the high-performance Mach 1 Mustangs of old. Consistent with past convention, the high-performance version will have a GT badge and be capable of 0–60 mph in around 3.5 seconds, which is as quick as the flagship gas-powered Mustang Shelby GT500.

The Mach-E is arguably Tesla-inspired, with its large cockpit display, front-end styling, and panoramic sunroof. It is about the same size as a Ford Escape or Porsche Macan. The interior is modern, including cutting-edge infotainment options. Its two battery options include a 75.7 kWh standard range and a 98.8 kWh extended range. All models will have fast-charging capability so drivers can add up to sixty-one miles of range in just ten minutes. Through a recent partnership, Ford will provide fast-charging stations across the US.

| | |
|---|---|
| Starting Price (MSRP) | $44,995 |
| Range (miles) | 230/310 |
| Availability | Late 2020 |
| Vehicle Class | Crossover SUV |
| Zero to 60 mph (secs) | Low 6 to mid-3 |
| Horsepower | 266–459 |
| Battery (kWh) | 68/88 |
| Cargo Area (ft3) | 64.4 |
| Length (in) | 186 |
| Drive (FWD, RWD, AWD) | RWD/AWD |
| Weight (lbs) | 4,394 |
| Basic Warranty | 3-Year, 36,000 Miles |
| Battery Warranty | 8-Year, 100,000 Miles |

## Hyundai Ioniq Electric

Often compared to the Chevrolet Bolt, Kia Niro EV, and Nissan LEAF, the Hyundai Ioniq Electric is one of the most affordable EVs. It is the pure EV version of Hyundai's popular gas-powered Ioniq compact hatchback.

The 2020 model year received a larger battery and stronger motor. The Ioniq Electric now has a 134-horsepower motor with a 38.3 kWh battery, giving it 170 miles of drive range. It also received an upgrade in its charging system. It can now charge to 80 percent in less than an hour with 100 kW fast-charging.

The Ioniq Electric is available in two trim levels, the SE and Limited. The SE trim level seems to be the best value. If you can afford more, it is probably a better choice to move up to the Hyundai Kona Electric, which has more range, power, and room.

The Ioniq Electric SE is a solid offering with features like keyless entry and ignition, Apple CarPlay, Android Auto, and adaptive cruise control. The Limited adds features like LED headlights, a sunroof, leather upholstery, navigation, a larger touchscreen, and an eight-speaker audio system.

| | |
|---|---|
| Starting Price (MSRP) | $33,045 |
| Range (miles) | 170 |
| Availability | Started Shipping 2016 |
| Units Sold in US | Less than 20,000 |
| Vehicle Class | Compact Hatchback |
| NHTSA Safety Rating (5-star) | Not Rated |
| NCAP Safety Rating (5-star) | Not Rated |
| Zero to 60 MPH (secs) | 11.4 |
| Horsepower | 134 |
| Battery (kWh) | 38.3 |
| Cargo Area (ft3) | 23 |
| Length (in) | 176 |
| Drive (FWD, RWD, AWD) | FWD |
| Weight (lbs) | 3,164 |
| Basic Warranty | 5-Year, 60,000 Miles |
| Battery Warranty | 10-Year, 100,000 Miles |

## Hyundai Kona Electric

The Kona Electric is a decent non-luxury crossover SUV with good range and a mid-market price. Although it is offered in three trim levels, you probably won't be disappointed with the base SEL level. All levels have a 64 kWh battery and a 201-horsepower motor driving the front wheels (all-wheel drive is not available).

The base SEL model includes a DC fast-charging port, Apple CarPlay, and Android Auto. Paying the premium for the Limited or the Ultimate gets you extra luxury and tech features. The Limited is the mid-level, and it provides features that are standard in most luxury EVs, including LED headlights, leather upholstery, a sunroof, and a power-adjustable driver's seat. The Ultimate is the top trim level and includes a bigger ten-inch touchscreen, navigation, a head-up display, an eight-speaker Infinity sound system, adaptive cruise control, and forward-collision mitigation. The Limited trim level seems to deliver the best value and comes close to matching the feature set in competitive electric SUVs.

One potential downside is that the Kona Electric was not specifically designed to be an EV. Hyundai swapped the Kona SUV's gas engine for a motor and battery to create the Kona Electric. That said, Hyundai's engineers designed a decent regenerative braking system that enables true one-pedal driving.

| | |
|---|---|
| Starting Price (MSRP) | $37,190 |
| Range (miles) | 258 |
| Availability | Started Shipping 2019 |
| Units Sold in US | Fewer than 100,000 |
| Vehicle Class | Crossover SUV |
| NHTSA Safety Rating (5-star) | Not Rated |
| Zero to 60 mph (secs) | 6.4 |
| Horsepower | 201 |
| Battery (kWh) | 64 |
| Cargo Area (ft3) | 19 |
| Length (in) | 165 |
| Drive (FWD, RWD, AWD) | FWD |
| Weight (lbs) | 3,767 |
| Basic Warranty | 10-Year, 100,000 Miles |
| Battery Warranty | 10-Year, 100,000 Miles |

## Jaguar I-PACE

After its 2018 launch, the Jaguar I-PACE became one of the most decorated cars of all time. It won the 2019 World Car of the Year and the European Car of the Year award (the only Jaguar to win this latter award).

After Tesla's Model X, Jaguar was the next company to introduce a luxury SUV, beating Audi and Mercedes-Benz to market. The I-PACE is stylish and comfortable. Its brisk all-wheel drive (AWD) acceleration from two motors and its handling can make you feel like you are driving a sports car. However, letting up on the accelerator doesn't invoke aggressive regenerative breaking, so one-pedal driving isn't as effective as it is for its competitors.

The I-PACE comes in three trim levels, S, SE, and HSE. The mid-level SE seems to be the best value with its added twenty-inch wheels, leather upholstery, and brighter LED headlights. Its fast-charging capability has been improved for 2021. Buyers considering an I-PACE should be aware that US sales during the first half of 2020 have been disappointing, with only about 1,400 units sold. Some reports suggest that this is due to competitive shortcomings like its true range and less refined user interface.

| | |
|---|---|
| Starting Price (MSRP) | $69,850 |
| Range (miles) | 234 |
| Availability | Started Shipping 2018 |
| Units Sold in US | Fewer than 7,000 |
| Vehicle Class | Luxury SUV |
| NHTSA Safety Rating (5-star) | Not Rated |
| NCAP Safety Rating (5-star) | 5/5 |
| Zero to 60 mph (secs) | 4.5 |
| Horsepower | 394 |
| Battery (kWh) | 90 |
| Cargo Area (ft3) | 25.3 |
| Length (in) | 184 |
| Drive (FWD, RWD, AWD) | AWD |
| Weight (lbs) | 4,784 |
| Basic Warranty | 5-Year, 60,000 Miles |
| Battery Warranty | 8-Year, 100,000 Miles |

## Kia Niro EV

Although not identical to the Hyundai Kona EV, the Kia Niro EV is its corporate sibling. They are the only two non-luxury electric crossover SUVs on the US market today. The Niro is a little larger and more expensive than the Kona. It will be eligible for the $7,500 US federal tax credit for some time. Both models have the same 64 kWh battery, 201-horsepower electric motor, and FWD configuration. AWD isn't available, despite the SUV styling.

The Niro EV is offered in two trim levels, the EX and the EX Premium. The EX looks to be a good choice because it comes with a lot of standard features, such as heated front seats and adaptive cruise control. EX Premium adds luxury features, including a premium sound system and sunroof.

The Niro isn't specifically designed as an EV, as Kia also sells it as a hybrid and plug-in hybrid. It has a roomy interior and looks like a normal SUV. Its range, price, and quick acceleration make the Niro EV one of the top-ranked EVs and it is definitely worth checking out.

| | |
|---|---|
| Starting Price (MSRP) | $39,090 |
| Range (miles) | 239 |
| Availability | Started Shipping 2018 |
| Units Sold in US | Fewer than 5,000 |
| Vehicle Class | Crossover SUV |
| NHTSA Safety Rating (5-star) | Not Rated |
| NCAP Safety Rating (5-star) | Not Rated |
| Zero to 60 mph (secs) | 6.2 |
| Horsepower | 201 |
| Battery (kWh) | 64 |
| Cargo Area (ft3) | 18.5 |
| Length (in) | 172 |
| Drive (FWD, RWD, AWD) | FWD |
| Weight (lbs) | 3,854 |
| Basic Warranty | 10-Year, 100,000 Miles |
| Battery Warranty | 10-Year, 100,000 Miles |

## Lordstown Endurance

Lordstown Motors Corporation is a new EV spinoff of Workhorse Group Incorporated, a company based in Cincinnati, Ohio, which specializes in the manufacturing of electric delivery and utility vehicles. In November 2019, Lordstown Motors acquired the 6.2 million square foot General Motors Lordstown plant in Lordstown, Ohio. The first vehicle manufactured here will be the Endurance. The Endurance is expected to first be available to fleet customers in mid-2021, with mass-market customer deliveries starting later in the year. The Endurance will be powered by four motors. Like the Rivian, one motor will be mounted in each hub. The combined power from all four motors is expected to be more than six hundred horsepower. This design gives better power and braking control for each wheel.

| | |
|---|---|
| Starting Price (MSRP) | $52,5000 |
| Range (miles) | 250+ |
| Availability | Estimated 2021 |
| Vehicle Class | Light-Duty Pickup Truck |
| NHTSA Safety Rating (5-star) | Not Rated |
| NCAP Safety Rating (5-star) | Not Rated |
| Horsepower | 600 |
| Drive (FWD, RWD, AWD) | AWD |
| Basic Warranty | 3-Year Bumper-to-Bumper |
| Battery Warranty | 8-Year, 100,000 Miles |

## Lucid Air

Originally called Atieva, Lucid Motors was founded in 2007. Their original focus was building electric vehicle batteries and powertrains to be sold to other manufacturers. They also supplied batteries to Formula E racing. Coinciding with a business pivot that focused development on an all-electric luxury performance vehicle, the company changed its name to Lucid Motors in October 2016.

Its headquarters is in Newark, California, and they are building a manufacturing plant in Casa Grande, Arizona. In April 2020, Lucid announced that it had closed a more than $1 billion investment from the Public Investment Fund of Saudi Arabia.

Expected in late 2021 and positioned to compete with the Tesla Model S, its flagship vehicle will be a full-size luxury sedan called the Lucid Air. With a starting price of about $80,000, the Air is expected to be available in single motor and dual-motor configurations, with two choices of batteries. Its top version is expected to have a 0–60 mph time of 2.5 seconds and a 400-mile range. Some of its luxury features will include a panoramic sunroof, large executive seats in the rear, and a premium sound system with noise cancelation.

Like several other EV manufacturers, Lucid Motors will offer nationwide charging through an agreement with Electrify America.

| | |
|---|---|
| Starting Price (MSRP) | Appx. $79,995 |
| Range (miles) | 400–500+ |
| Availability | Estimated Mid 2021 |
| Vehicle Class | Fullsize Luxury Sedan |
| NHTSA Safety Rating (5-star) | Not Rated |
| NCAP Safety Rating (5-star) | Not Rated |
| Zero to 60 MPH (secs) | 2.5 |
| Horsepower | 620-1080 |
| Battery (kWh) | 75/113 |
| Cargo Area (ft3) | 26 |
| Length (in) | 196 |
| Drive (FWD, RWD, AWD) | RWD/AWD |

## Mercedes-Benz EQC

The EQC is the first Mercedes-Benz EV and the first of their EQ "electrified" sub-brand. EQC batteries are manufactured by a wholly owned subsidiary in the Daimler AG family, which represents a commitment to EVs and an indication that more Mercedes EVs will follow. To fulfill European orders first, Mercedes delayed the EQC's US launch date to 2021. That delay will make it the fourth entry in its class, competing against the Audi e-tron, Jaguar I-PACE, and Tesla Model X.

The EQC is a small SUV about the same size as the current GLC. Mercedes states a range of 279 miles, but that range is based on European testing. EPA tests tend to come in lower. The EQC should test out to an EPA range greater than 200 miles.

It has two motors that drive the axles separately and is powered by an 80 kWh battery. Because Mercedes took extra steps to insulate the cabin, the EQC is expected to have a very quiet interior.

It is available in three trim levels: Progressive, Premium, and Advanced. Advanced offers three paint and upholstery options, while Progressive and Premium offer two. All models have a sunroof to let in natural light. As expected from this brand, the quality of materials is impeccable. The EQC comes standard with SiriusXM satellite radio and a Burmester audio system.

| Starting Price (MSRP) | To Be Announced |
|---|---|
| Range (miles) | 277 |
| Availability | Expected 2021 |
| Vehicle Class | Luxury SUV |
| NHTSA Safety Rating (5-star) | Not Rated |
| NCAP Safety Rating (5-star) | 5/5 |
| Zero to 60 mph (secs) | 4.8 |
| Horsepower | 402 |
| Battery (kWh) | 80 |
| Cargo Area (ft3) | TBA |
| Length (in) | 187 |
| Drive (FWD, RWD, AWD) | AWD |
| Weight (lbs) | TBA |
| Basic Warranty | 4-Year, 50,000 Miles |
| Battery Warranty | 8-Year, 100,000 Miles |

## MINI Cooper Electric

When it launched in 1969, the original MINI Cooper created a new automotive segment. It was a utilitarian city car. BMW acquired the MINI brand and launched a modernized, more luxurious MINI in 2001. With its BMW DNA, it was quicker and sportier.

The 2021 MINI Cooper Electric puts yet another twist on the concept. It will retain the quirkiness and handling of its predecessor while adding the instant response of an EV. This will be MINI's first electric production car.

Some of its interesting features include dual-zone automatic climate-control system and a special heat-pump design that uses 75 percent less energy than a traditional electric heater. Its below-average range and two-door body style will limit its appeal to the mass market, but it is a great option if you are looking for a fun commuter EV.

| | |
|---|---|
| Starting Price (MSRP) | $29,900 |
| Range (miles) | 110 |
| Availability | Estimated Late 2020 |
| Vehicle Class | Subcompact |
| NHTSA Safety Rating (5-star) | Not Rated |
| NCAP Safety Rating (5-star) | 4/5 |
| Zero to 60 mph (secs) | 6.9 |
| Horsepower | 184 |
| Battery (kWh) | 32.6 |
| Cargo Area (ft3) | 7.5 |
| Length (in) | 151 |
| Drive (FWD, RWD, AWD) | FWD |
| Weight (lbs) | 3,153 |
| Basic Warranty | 4-Year, 50,000 Miles |
| Battery Warranty | 8-Year, 100,000 Miles |

## Nissan Ariya

Expected to be available in late 2021, the Ariya represents Nissan's modern EV reboot. Its smoother lines are a departure from Nissan's typical sharp, angular look.

The modern upgrade continues inside with a Tesla-inspired minimalistic dash. Nissan went with two wide touchscreens embedded in the dash, which look a bit like Mercedes-Benz's MBUX infotainment system.

The Ariya will be offered with two battery sizes, 63 kWh and 87 kWh. Front-wheel drive will be standard, but dual-motor AWD will be available with both battery sizes. Horsepower is expected to be between 215 and 389, depending on battery type and FWD versus AWD.

The Ariya is expected to support fast charging up to 130 kW, which should charge it to 80 percent in about twenty minutes. We expect the acceleration of the AWD version with a high-capacity battery to be 0–60 mph in less than 5.0 seconds. It will have an e-pedal, like the LEAF, which will enable one-pedal driving.

| Starting Price (MSRP) | Approximately $40,000 |
|---|---|
| Range (miles) | Appx. 220/300 |
| Availability | Estimated Late 2021 |
| Vehicle Class | Crossover SUV |
| Zero to 60 mph (secs) | Estimated < 5.0 (AWD) |
| Horsepower | 215/389 |
| Battery (kWh) | 63/87 |
| Cargo Area (ft3) | 16.5 (AWD version) |
| Drive (FWD, RWD, AWD) | FWD/AWD |
| Basic Warranty | 5-Year, 60,000 Miles |

## Nissan LEAF

The Nissan LEAF launched the mass market for EVs in 2011. Nissan deserves credit for starting the electric car surge. The LEAF isn't the most exciting EV, but it is roomy and relatively affordable. It is typically compared to the Chevrolet Bolt, Kia Niro EV, and Hyundai Ioniq Electric. The LEAF has continued to improve, and its second generation was launched in 2018.

It is available in two versions. The base has a 147-horsepower motor with a 40 kWh battery, giving it a 150-mile range. The LEAF Plus has a 214-horsepower motor with a 62 kWh battery and a range of 226 miles.

The LEAF is offered in three trim levels, the S, SV, and SL. All models come with an upgraded eight-inch infotainment display, Apple CarPlay, and Android Auto. The S and SV interiors have an economy-car feel. However, stepping up to the SL level gives you a seven-speaker Bose audio system and an optional gray leather interior with matching dash pad.

Of the three, the SV trim level looks like the best value, with its fast charging, adaptive cruise control, and better audio system and navigation. The all-weather package available with the SV can improve efficiency in cold climates. Its heated front seats and steering wheel can help you feel warm without heating the whole cabin.

| | |
|---|---|
| Starting Price (MSRP) | $31,600 |
| Range (miles) | 149/226 |
| Availability | Started Shipping 2011 |
| Units Sold in US | Fewer than 200,000 |
| Vehicle Class | Compact Hatchback |
| NHTSA Safety Rating (5-star) | 4/5 (2014 model) |
| NCAP Safety Rating (5-star) | 5/5 |
| Zero to 60 mph (secs) | Appx. 7.5 (standard) |
| Horsepower | 147/214 |
| Battery (kWh) | 40/62 |
| Cargo Area (ft3) | 23.6 |
| Length (in) | 176 |
| Drive (FWD, RWD, AWD) | FWD |
| Weight (lbs) | 3,538 |
| Basic Warranty | 5-Year, 60,000 Miles |
| Battery Warranty | 8-Year, 100,000 Miles |

## Polestar 2

Polestar is a subsidiary of Volvo Cars. It is headquartered in Gothenburg, Sweden, with vehicle production in China.

Of all the electric cars released to date, only the Tesla Model 3 is classified as a midsize sedan. The Polestar 2 will be the second, and although it is priced at a significant premium, the Polestar 2 looks to be positioned as a direct competitor to the Tesla Model 3.

The Polestar 2 has a total of 405-horsepower from two motors, with a 78 kWh battery for 275 miles of driving range. The interior is minimalistic, with a stylish Scandinavian-inspired design made from vegan materials. Polestar opted to go with a Google-powered infotainment system on an eleven-inch touchscreen that integrates Google Maps and Google Assistant. The audio system is Harman/Kardon.

Options are a la carte and limited to a Performance package, upgraded leather upholstery, twenty-inch wheels and metallic paint. Similar to Tesla's introduction strategy, Polestar is expected to only sell the high-priced versions, with more basic models becoming available over time.

| | |
|---|---|
| Starting Price (MSRP) | $61,200 |
| Range (miles) | 275 |
| Availability | Late 2020 |
| Vehicle Class | Midsize Sedan |
| NHTSA Safety Rating (5-star) | Not Rated |
| NCAP Safety Rating (5-star) | Not Rated |
| Zero to 60 mph (secs) | 4.7 |
| Horsepower | 405 |
| Battery (kWh) | 78 |
| Length (in) | 181 |
| Drive (FWD, RWD, AWD) | AWD |
| Basic Warranty | 4-Year, 50,000 Miles |
| Battery Warranty | 8-Year, 100,000 Miles |

## Porsche Taycan

Although priced at the very top of mass-market EVs, the Taycan delivers the performance, styling, and build quality that is expected from the Porsche brand. Whether an EV or not, it is a beautiful car.

Size-wise, the Taycan is a four-door sedan with a shape reminiscent of a 911 and a smaller dimensions than the Panamera. With a 0–60 mph time of 2.6 seconds, the Taycan's top trim level and optional high-capacity battery make it one of the fastest accelerating EVs on the market. However, at 192 miles, the range is adequate but not extraordinary. The range is about half of the Tesla Model S's, which is its main competition.

The Taycan is offered in three trim levels, the 4S, Turbo, and Turbo S. It has a standard 79.2 kWh battery and an optional upgrade to a 93.4 kWh battery. Because Porsche wants the Taycan to feel like a gas-powered car, its regenerative braking isn't noticeable to the driver, and one-pedal driving is unavailable. The Taycan uses regenerative breaking to augment, not replace, the traditional braking system.

Another impressive feature is the Taycan's fast charging. It can recharge from an empty battery to full in about twenty-two minutes. However, this is only possible at high-powered Electrify America stations.

| | |
|---|---|
| Starting Price (MSRP) | $103,800 |
| Range (miles) | 192 |
| Availability | Started Shipping 2019 |
| Units Sold in US | Fewer than 1,000 |
| Vehicle Class | Midsize Sedan |
| NHTSA Safety Rating (5-star) | Not Rated |
| NCAP Safety Rating (5-star) | 5/5 |
| Zero to 60 mph (secs) | 3.8 – 2.6 |
| Horsepower | 522–750 |
| Battery (kWh) | 79.2/93.4 kWh |
| Cargo Area (ft3) | 17 |
| Length (in) | 195 |
| Drive (FWD, RWD, AWD) | AWD |
| Weight (lbs) | 4,777–5,132 |
| Basic Warranty | 4-Year, 50,000 Miles |
| Battery Warranty | 8-Year, 100,000 Miles |

# Rivian R1T

Rivian Automotive LLC is an electric-vehicle startup founded in 2009 with headquarters in Plymouth, Michigan. It operates a manufacturing plant in Normal, Illinois, and a battery facility in Irvine, California. Like Tesla has already done, Rivian is one of very few EV startups that will go into production.

Rivian has raised over $1.5 billion from investors, including $700 million from Amazon, $500 million from Ford Motor Company, and $350 million from Cox automotive. In addition to EVs, their products include chassis with batteries that they intend to sell to other automotive manufacturers.

In late-2018, Rivian announced the names of their first two vehicles, the R1T pickup truck and the R1S SUV. Both are designed for off-road use and have an impressive fourteen inches of ground clearance.

Rivian plans to offer three battery sizes for three different ranges. The R1T is a midsize crew-cab pickup truck. The interior is stylish, with wood trim and two large touch-screen displays—one in front of the driver and one in the middle of the dash.

The R1T has significant differentiation from other EVs, including a true off-road suspension and impressive towing capacity.

Also, the Rivian powertrain is designed with four motors, one on each wheel. Four motors should deliver very precise traction control. Another innovation is the R1T gear tunnel, which is a large, lockable space that runs behind the cab.

| | |
|---|---|
| Starting Price (MSRP) | Approximately $70,500 |
| Range (miles) | 230–400+ |
| Availability | Late 2020 |
| Vehicle Class | Mid-Size Crew Cab Pickup |
| NHTSA Safety Rating (5-star) | Not Rated |
| NCAP Safety Rating (5-star) | Not Rated |
| Zero to 60 mph (secs) | 4.9 – 3.2 |
| Horsepower | Up to 750 |
| Battery (kWh) | 105/135/180 |
| Length (in) | 217 |
| Drive (FWD, RWD, AWD) | AWD |
| Weight (lbs) | 5,886 |

## Rivian **R1S**

The R1S is a seven-passenger SUV built by Rivian Automotive. For more info about Rivian, see the R1T guide.

The R1S is positioned to compete against the Tesla Model X, making it the second three-row electric SUV on the market. It will share the same chassis, motor, and battery configuration as the R1T.

Customers will be able to buy the R1S directly from Rivian. Rivian plans to copy Tesla's model of nationwide service centers. The R1S will have an air suspension, making it possible for drivers to change their ground clearance. The cabin's leather and wood trim are beautiful. Like the R1T, the R1S will have two large touchscreen displays, one in front of the driver and one in the middle of the dash.

| | |
|---|---|
| Starting Price (MSRP) | Approximately $70,500 |
| Range (miles) | 240–410 |
| Availability | Early 2021 |
| Vehicle Class | Off-Road SUV |
| Zero to 60 mph (secs) | 4.9 – 3.2 |
| Horsepower | Up to 750 |
| Battery (kWh) | 105/135/180 |
| Length (in) | 201 |
| Drive (FWD, RWD, AWD) | AWD |
| Weight (lbs) | 5,842 |

# Tesla Model S

When the Tesla Model S launched in 2012, it changed the world. It was stylish, luxurious, and had a long driving range. It has continued to improve, and traditional automakers have failed to catch it.

With its early build-quality issues resolved, the Model S continues to set the bar as one of the preeminent electric cars. It is even more impressive today with its industry-leading estimated range of 402 miles. The interior has understated styling and uses quality materials. However, we do find it odd that it doesn't integrate either Apple CarPlay or Android Auto.

The Model S's air suspension gives it a comfortable, rather than sporty, ride. It is available in two variants, Long Range Plus and Performance. Both are dual-motor AWD and have the same 100 kWh battery.

Tesla puts a high priority on safety. A suite of features is included with its Autopilot system, including parking sensors, blind-spot monitoring, lane-departure warning, and forward-collision warning with braking.

The Model S's performance is now legendary, with the base model going from 0–60 mph in just 3.7 seconds. Stepping up to the Performance model reduces the 0–60 time to a supercar 2.3 seconds. The Performance model also comes with an upgraded interior and a carbon-fiber spoiler.

Tesla's Full Self-Driving Capability is optional on both models. It includes automatic highway lane changes, assisted stops at traffic-controlled intersections, and automated parking. The Model S has full access to Tesla's Supercharger network.

| | |
|---|---|
| Starting Price (MSRP) | $74,990 |
| Range (miles) | 402 |
| Availability | Started Shipping 2012 |
| Units Sold in US | Fewer than 170,000 |
| Vehicle Class | Fullsize Luxury Sedan |
| NHTSA Safety Rating (5-star) | 5/5 |
| NCAP Safety Rating (5-star) | 5/5 |
| Zero to 60 mph (secs) | 3.7 – 2.3 |
| Horsepower | 259/794 |
| Battery (kWh) | 100 |
| Cargo Area (ft3) | 28 |
| Length (in) | 196 |
| Drive (FWD, RWD, AWD) | AWD |
| Weight (lbs) | 4,883 |
| Basic Warranty | 4-Year, 50,000 Miles |
| Battery Warranty | 8-Year, Unlimited Miles |

## Tesla Model X

Tesla was the first to launch an all-electric luxury SUV in 2015. The Jaguar I-PACE and Audi e-tron soon followed, and the Mercedes-Benz EQC is expected to join this small field in 2021. However, there still isn't anything quite like the Model X, with its over 300-mile range and unique folding falcon-wing doors.

Its falcon-wing doors undoubtedly lend it a cool aesthetic, but they are of questionable practicality on an SUV. The folding doors make it impossible to install a traditional roof rack, and they cannot fully open if the vehicle is parked below a low ceiling.

The Model X shares the same chassis and drivetrain as the Model S. It is available in two variants and three seat configurations. Both variants, the Long Range Plus and the Performance, are dual-motor AWD and have the same 100 kWh battery.

The Model X comes standard with five-passenger seating. Optional six-passenger seating includes two captain's chairs in the second row and a bench in the third. The third seating arrangement is a seven-passenger configuration with two rows of benches. All seats are heated, as is the steering wheel.

Tesla's Full Self-Driving Capability is optional on both models. It includes automatic highway lane changes, assisted stops at traffic-controlled intersections, and automated parking. The Model X has full access to Tesla's Supercharger network—a huge advantage.

| Starting Price (MSRP) | $79,990 |
|---|---|
| Range (miles) | 351 |
| Availability | Started Shipping 2015 |
| Units Sold in US | Fewer than 100,000 |
| Vehicle Class | Luxury SUV |
| NHTSA Safety Rating (5-star) | 5/5 |
| NCAP Safety Rating (5-star) | 5/5 |
| Zero to 60 mph (secs) | 4.4 – 2.6 |
| Horsepower | 534/778 |
| Battery (kWh) | 100 |
| Cargo Area (ft3) | 88 |
| Length (in) | 198 |
| Drive (FWD, RWD, AWD) | AWD |
| Weight (lbs) | 5,531 |
| Basic Warranty | 4-Year, 50,000 Miles |
| Battery Warranty | 8-Year, 150,000 Miles |

# Tesla Model 3

True superlatives can be used to describe the Tesla Model 3. It is the safest car ever tested by the National Highway Traffic Safety Administration (NHTSA) in its forty-nine-year history. It was the best-selling car in California during the first quarter of 2020, displacing the much cheaper Honda Civic for the top spot.

The Model 3 is now in its fourth model year. Before COVID-19, at the end of 2019, Tesla was making more than 25,000 a month, achieving true mass-market quantities.

Tesla's mission is to deliver affordable EVs to the mass market. The modern touchscreen it uses in all its vehicles helps achieve this goal. Not having to design, produce, and install the fifty or so individual knobs and buttons that a traditional car has significantly reduces cost and delivers a clean, uncluttered cockpit.

The Model 3 comes in three trim levels, Standard Range Plus, Long Range, and Performance. Standard Range Plus is RWD with a 250-mile range, glass roof, and power-adjustable front seats. Long Range has dual-motor AWD with a larger 322-mile-range battery and a premium sound system. The Performance package has faster acceleration, heavier duty brakes, and a lower racing suspension.

The Autopilot safety suite with external cameras is standard on all models. Tesla's Full Self-Driving Capability option is available with all trim levels. Another huge advantage is access to Tesla's Supercharger network.

| Starting Price (MSRP) | $37,990 |
|---|---|
| Range (miles) | 250/322 |
| Availability | Started Shipping 2017 |
| Units Sold in US | Fewer than 400,000 |
| Vehicle Class | Luxury Midsize Sedan |
| NHTSA Safety Rating (5-star) | 5/5 |
| NCAP Safety Rating (5-star) | 5/5 |
| Zero to 60 mph (secs) | 5.3 – 3.2 |
| Horsepower | 283/450 |
| Battery (kWh) | 54/75 |
| Cargo Area (ft3) | 15 |
| Length (in) | 184 |
| Drive (FWD, RWD, AWD) | RWD/AWD |
| Weight (lbs) | 3,552 |
| Basic Warranty | 4-Year, 50,000 Miles |
| Battery Warranty | 8-Year, 120,000 Miles |

## Tesla Model Y

The Model Y is the latest model to be released by Tesla. It looks like a taller version of the Tesla Model 3, but with significantly more cargo space.

The Model Y is available in two trim levels, Long Range and Performance. Both are dual-motor AWD and have the same 75 kWh battery. Long Range includes nineteen-inch wheels, a panoramic glass roof, and a fourteen-speaker premium sound system. The Performance level has twenty-one-inch wheels, a lower racing suspension, and heavier duty brakes.

The driving range of the Model Y is rated by the EPA at 316 miles. Driving at highway speeds of 70 mph, the range drops to 276 miles.

Standard on both models is the Autopilot safety suite, which includes external cameras that enable functions like forward-collision mitigation (emergency braking), collision warning, and blind-spot monitoring. Tesla's Full Self-Driving Capability option is available with both trim levels.

Although the Model Y shares many parts with the Model 3, including the chassis and powertrain, one big difference is its cabin heating system. The Model Y is the first Tesla vehicle to use a heat pump instead of electric-resistance heating. The heat pump is expected to use two-thirds less battery energy than electric-resistance heating. That will improve the Model Y's driving range in cold weather. Both models can access Tesla's Supercharger network.

| Starting Price (MSRP) | $49,990 |
|---|---|
| Range (miles) | 316 |
| Availability | March 2020 |
| Units Sold in US | - |
| Vehicle Class | Luxury Crossover SUV |
| NHTSA Safety Rating (5-star) | Not Rated |
| NCAP Safety Rating (5-star) | Not Rated |
| Zero to 60 mph (secs) | 4.8 – 3.5 |
| Horsepower | 384/450 |
| Battery (kWh) | 75 |
| Cargo Area (ft3) | 68 |
| Length (in) | 187 |
| Drive (FWD, RWD, AWD) | AWD |
| Weight (lbs) | 4,416 |
| Basic Warranty | 4-Year, 50,000 Miles |
| Battery Warranty | 8-Year, 120,000 Miles |

## Tesla Roadster 2.0

Back in 2008, the original Tesla Roadster was launched to make a point. According to an August 2006 Tesla blog post, it was designed to beat a gasoline sports car like a Porsche or Ferrari in a head-to-head showdown, thus proving the viability of electric cars to the world. Production was halted after 2,500 units, but profits from its sales went on to fund development of subsequent Tesla models.

A new Tesla Roadster is expected to start shipping in 2021. It too is intended to make a bold, transformational statement. On June 10, 2018, Elon Musk tweeted, "Intent of new Tesla Roadster is to beat gas sports cars on every performance metric by far, no exceptions, thus transferring the "halo crown" effect gas cars have as the top speed leaders over to pure electric." The projected performance figures are supercar stunning.

The Roadster is expected to achieve a world record 0-60 mph time of 1.9 seconds. It will be powered by three motors with a 200 kWh battery for 620 miles of range. With this performance, the Roadster is a steal at $200,000.

By comparison, with a 0–60 mph time of 2.3 seconds, the Bugatti Chiron is the only gas-powered car that comes close to the Roadster's acceleration. However, the Chiron costs approximately fifteen times the price of the Tesla Roadster. As with other Tesla models, it will have access to Tesla's Supercharger network.

| Starting Price (MSRP) | Approximately $200,000 |
|---|---|
| Range (miles) | 620 |
| Availability | Expected 2021 |
| Vehicle Class | Supercar |
| NHTSA Safety Rating (5-star) | Not Rated |
| NCAP Safety Rating (5-star) | Not Rated |
| Zero to 60 mph (secs) | 1.9 |
| Battery (kWh) | 200 |
| Length (in) | 155 |
| Drive (FWD, RWD, AWD) | AWD |

## TESLA CYBERTRUCK

Unveiled in November 2019, the Cybertruck is another bold move by Tesla. Like the new Tesla Roadster and Semi, the Cybertruck is a completely reimagined vehicle representing an all-out attack on the status quo.

The Cybertruck's body has angular, sharp edges for a reason. Made from stamped body panels, traditional trucks have used a body-on-frame architecture for almost a hundred years. Tesla's Cybertruck design has a unibody, or exoskeleton, where the outer skin acts as the vehicle's frame. This is the difference between a bird and a bug.

The Cybertruck exoskeleton is made from a specialized cold-rolled stainless-steel alloy that is both stiff and light. It has a smooth surface that won't rust, so it doesn't need to be painted.

With its combined body and chassis and with no need for paint, the manufacturing costs are drastically reduced. This helps explain the Cybertruck's impressive value.

It has the strong angular shape because the body's ultra-hard steel can't be stamped—it has to be bent into shape. Drive this truck home and expect your neighbors to crowd around your driveway.

Scheduled to start shipping late in 2021, the Cybertruck will be offered in three versions: base single-motor RWD, dual-motor AWD, and tri-motor AWD. The cabin is minimalistic and spacious, with a panoramic glass roof. The Cybertruck will have best-in-class payload and towing capacity, another indication of its impressive value. The bed has a cargo capacity of one hundred cubic feet and is rated for 3,500-pound loads. This beast has an adjustable air suspension.

| | |
|---|---|
| Starting Price (MSRP) | $39,900 |
| Range (miles) | 250–500+ |
| Availability | Late 2021 |
| Vehicle Class | Full-Size Crew Cab Pickup |
| NHTSA Safety Rating (5-star) | Not Rated |
| NCAP Safety Rating (5-star) | Not Rated |
| Zero to 60 mph (secs) | 6.5 – 2.9 |
| Horsepower | TBA |
| Battery (kWh) | TBA |
| Length (in) | 232 |
| Drive (FWD, RWD, AWD) | RWD/AWD |
| Weight (lbs) | TBA |
| Basic Warranty | 4-Year, 50,000 Miles |
| Battery Warranty | 8-Year, Unlimited Miles |

## Volkswagen ID.4

The ID.4 is an electric SUV from Volkswagen for the US market. Initially, it will be RWD from a single rear-mounted motor. An AWD variant is expected later. Range is expected to be up to 310 miles.

Classified as a non-luxury compact SUV, the ID.4 fills a niche and represents the downward trend in EV prices. It will be the first non-luxury SUV, larger than the Hyundai Kona Electric and Kia Niro EV, and comparable in size to the Tesla Model Y, but less expensive.

The ID.4 will probably have an interior similar to the ID.3, which started shipping to the European market in 2019. If so, it will have few physical buttons or knobs and instead utilize voice-activated controls and several touchscreen displays. The ID.3 and ID.4 use the same modular MEB platform for electric cars that was designed by Volkswagen Group.

| Starting Price (MSRP) | Approximately $35,000 |
|---|---|
| Range (miles) | Approximately 310 |
| Availability | Expected 2021 |
| Vehicle Class | Compact SUV |
| NHTSA Safety Rating (5-star) | Not Rated |
| NCAP Safety Rating (5-star) | Not Rated |
| Drive (FWD, RWD, AWD) | RWD |

## Notable Exceptions

**BMW iX3**: On March 8, 2020, BMW canceled its plan to launch the BMW iX3 in the US. This would have been its first new EV in years. A BMW spokesperson told Automotive News, "At this time, we do not have plans to bring the iX3 to the US market."

**Ford F-150 Electric**: During an interview on CNBC June 10, 2020, Ford's chief operating officer, Jim Farley, stated that the Ford F-150 EV will launch in mid-2022 along with the new Transit electric van. This is a slip from the "late 2020" release that Ford had previously stated.

**Kia Soul EV**: In October 2019, Kia announced that the Kia Soul EV would be delayed from the 2020 model year to the 2021 model year. Kia gave low motor and battery supplies as the reason for the delay. Now we are hearing that the Kia Soul EV will be canceled in the US. Kia has removed the Soul EV from its US website and almost all mention of it from its US media site.

**Smart EQ ForFour**: Part of the Mercedes-Benz's "EQ" sub-brand, the Smart EQ ForFour is the electric version of the Smart ForFour city car. In 2017, the Smart brand went all-electric in North America. This caused many US Mercedes-Benz dealerships to stop selling them. Smart is a division of Daimler AG. Smart has been unprofitable for several years. To resolve profitability issues, Daimler and Geely Holding entered a 50:50 joint venture in May 2019 to form a new entity, Smart Automobile Co., Ltd. The strategy is to make Smart a global all-electric brand. A new generation of cars is expected in 2022, with production to take place in China.

# OWNING AN EV

Owning an electric vehicle is a lot like owning a gas-powered vehicle, but some things are different. One is that you don't have to spend time at a gas station getting a fill-up. Of course, you can still stop to buy a bag of Doritos and be on your way without handling the gas pump.

Instead of filling up with gasoline, you need to charge your car. You can do that at home or at public charging stations. In this chapter, we cover a few items that you should consider when thinking about buying an EV.

## CHARGING

EV charging comes in three "levels." Level 1 and 2 can be performed from an owner's home or apartment. Level 3 requires a supply voltage that is typically only available in areas zoned as commercial.

Level 1 is the slowest way to charge an EV. It uses a standard 120-volt wall outlet. Level 1 charging typically adds about four miles of range per hour (RPH). Depending on the model of EV, it can take between eight and twenty-four hours to recharge the battery. Level 1 is convenient but slow. To charge faster, you need to use a higher voltage.

For peace of mind, keep a long extension cord in your trunk. We recommend a one-hundred-foot cord. That will allow you to recharge almost anywhere you go, even at campgrounds. As long as you can find a standard electrical outlet, you will be able to power your car.

Level 2 charging is typically what people install in their homes. It requires a 240-volt electric circuit—the same as is used for large electric appliances like dryers or stoves. Level 2 charging is typically six times faster than Level 1. Level 2 adds about twenty-five miles of driving range per hour. Most EVs come with a portable Level 2 charger that includes a 240-volt plug and a 120-volt plug so that it can also be used as a Level 1 charger. If your clothes dryer is near your garage, you can probably use that outlet for charging your EV.

A slightly more convenient and cleaner-looking option is to install a wall-mounted Level 2 charger. These range in price from about $180 for aftermarket units to $500 for units from your EV manufacturer. According to HomeAdvisor, it will cost you $1,200 to $2,000 to have a Level 2 charger professionally installed. This includes the parts and labor of installation but doesn't include the charger itself.

A typical wall-mounted Level 2 charger.

If you live in an apartment or are looking for an apartment, be sure to ask your landlord about EV charging stations and whether you will have access to a 220-volt outlet. If your apartment complex doesn't have EV charging, you can ask your landlord about having one installed. ChargePoint, one of the largest EV charging networks in the US, even offers a simple form letter that you can fill out and send to your landlord for them to request to have a charger installed. A public charger will increase the value of the rental property.

Level 3 provides even faster charging. It is also called DC fast charging. Level 3 requires a 480-volt electric circuit, which is typically only found in commercially zoned areas. It can usually recharge a battery up to 80 percent capacity in less than a half hour. The idea is that you plug in for about twenty minutes and grab a cup of coffee or snack while you charge.

Level 3 equipment is not compatible with all vehicles. For example, all Teslas and the Nissan LEAF can accept a Level 3 charge, but the Chevy Volt cannot. There is currently no industry standard for this level of charging. These chargers are being deployed across the United States in public and commercial settings, with Tesla being the only brand that has a coast-to-coast infrastructure already installed.

Public charging stations are becoming more common at grocery stores, libraries, and public and workplace parking lots. As we described in our Myths chapter, the number of public EV charging stations in the United States is growing rapidly. The United States now has more than 20,000 electric car charging stations with more than 90,000 connectors. Each charging station can have multiple connections. Two years ago, there were about 16,000 public electric vehicle charging stations with about 43,000 connectors. So, the expansion of stations has been about 38 percent in two years.

Charging stations like this one in front of Redmond, WA city hall, are now widely available.

The charging station market is currently led by three big players. Tesla claims to have 1,971 Supercharger Stations with 17,467 connectors, most positioned along major highways. Charge-Point has 30,000 connectors and Electrify America has 12,000 charging stations and 35,000 connectors. As you are driving in unfamiliar terrain, how do you find these connections? There are at least nine different Android and iOS apps to help you find public charging stations.

Tucked away in the corner of a parking lot, this charging station can be located by using a phone app.

> **Under the Hood:**
>
> *Electricity comes in two flavors: alternating current (AC) and direct current (DC). In the US, alternating current changes from positive to negative voltage and back again sixty times each second. In many other countries, the frequency of alternating current is fifty cycles per second instead of sixty. Direct current (DC) has a steady flow in one direction. In your home, the wall outlets supply AC power, while many of your smaller devices, say the TV remote control, use DC power supplied by batteries.*

With a few exceptions, electric vehicles typically come with one of four different types of plugs in their charging ports. Plug Types 1 and 2 are for AC charging. The CCS and CHAdeMo plug types are for DC. The type of plug isn't usually that important because most EVs come with a converter so that you can plug your EV into most types of charging connectors. For example, the Tesla Model 3 ships with a charge kit which contains a charging adaptor to convert from Type 2 (J1772) charger cables to the Type 1 used by Tesla.

> **Under the Hood:**
>
> *The funny name CHAdeMo is derived from the Japanese meaning: "How about a cup of tea?" The phrase suggests that your car will charge in about the time it takes to enjoy a cup of tea.*

| | |
|---|---|
| | **Type 1**<br><br>This is a 120 V plug that is standard for EVs from North America and Asia. It will allow you to charge up to 7.4 kW. Also called the J1772 or J-plug. |
| | **Type 2**<br><br>This is a triple-phase plug, meaning it provides 240 V. With three additional wires to let current run through, it can charge your car faster than Type 1. It will allow 22 kW charging at home and 43 kW at charging stations. |
| | **CCS**<br><br>CCS (Combined Charging System) is an enhanced version of the Type 1 plug with two additional power contacts, which enables it to perform fast charging at a speed of up to 350 kW. |
| | **CHAdeMo**<br><br>Developed in Japan, this system enables quick charging up to 100 kW. CHAdeMO is currently the only standardized charging protocol that supports vehicle-to-grid (V2G), which enables EVs to store and then return electricity to the grid that has been generated by private residences using renewable sources like solar and wind. This is a future vision that is currently in the development phase. |

## COST TO CHARGE

Compared to gas-powered vehicles, EVs are much cheaper to fill up. Charging at home takes advantage of the low cost of electric power. Most EV owners report a modest-to-unnoticeable increase in their electric bill. The average kW rate was $0.1282/kW in the United States during February 2020. This means that it will cost about $6.40 to charge an average-sized 50 kWh EV battery. Average monthly electric power bills in the US range from $100 to $165 per month.

If that EV with a 50 kWh battery gets a typical 200-mile range, it will cost about $3.20 to drive it 100 miles. As described above, a comparable gasoline-powered car will cost about 3½ times more.

You can save more money by taking advantage of off-peak discounts. Many utilities charge less for electric power during times of the day when usage is low. By charging at home at night, the cost for electricity will be lower. Your electric company can tell you what the rate difference is.

---

### Under the Hood:

*It costs a little over $3.00 to drive a typical EV one hundred miles. If your gasoline-powered car gets twenty-five miles per gallon, it takes four gallons to cover that distance. Gas prices fluctuate wildly anywhere from $2.50 per gallon to $4.00, so driving one hundred miles would cost you between $10 and $16. That's $3 versus $10 to $16.*

Discounts for electricity vary by the hour and the season. For example, as of July 2020, Los Angeles Department of Water and Power (LADWP) charges 38 percent more for peak power than for off-peak power. LADWP peak hours are 1:00 p.m. to 5:00 p.m. in the summer (June 1 to September 30). Their off-peak hours on weekdays are midnight to 10:00 a.m. and 8:00 p.m. to midnight. On weekends, off-peak is twenty-four hours a day. The discount in the winter is much lower.

Some cities have free public charging stations. Some places to look are malls, shopping centers, and libraries. You can use the PlugShare app to find free EV charging. Some Tesla models receive free Supercharging, while owners of other models have to pay a modest fee.

## Tax Credits and Incentives

The federal government and state governments offer tax credits, tax deductions, and other incentives that lower the cost of acquiring and operating an EV. The US Department of Energy's Alternative Fuel Data Center website lists programs by state.

The largest tax deduction is the $7,500 offered by the US federal government. However, only two hundred thousand vehicles from each carmaker qualify for this bonus. Tesla has exceeded its limit.

Eight states offer EV tax rebates, with Colorado offering the highest at $4,000. Many states and individual municipalities offer Electric Vehicle Supply Equipment grants, rebates, and other incentives. For example, Tuscon Electric Power offers a rebate to residential customers that covers up to 75 percent of the cost of installing a home charger.

## WARRANTY

US federal law mandates that EV battery warranties cover at least eight years or one hundred thousand miles for the batteries of all EVs sold in the US. However, the federal regulation only covers complete battery failure.

Excluding complete battery failure, companies offer a range of warranties. For example, BMW, Chevrolet, Nissan, Tesla (Model 3), and Volkswagen will replace a battery if it loses 30 to 40 percent of its capacity during the warranty period. Others may not. It is important to do your research before making a purchase.

## INSURANCE

According to NerdWallet, insurance premiums for electric vehicles can be 16 to 26 percent higher than for comparable internal-combustion-engine cars.

# FUTURE

Electric vehicles have reached market acceptance, and their future looks bright. Current sales growth projected into the future shows EVs taking a much bigger percentage of the car market.

Many governments, some with the largest populations and worst air quality, are mandating EVs. Concentrating on air pollution generated at power stations makes it easier to reduce overall pollution. Also, the green value of EVs will get greener as renewable energy powers more of the grid.

EV innovation is accelerating due to contributions from all around the globe, not just Silicon Valley. Improvements in batteries, motor control, and support software will continue to occur and will make EVs an even better investment. Improvements are coming in both driving range and speed.

Lastly, the good news isn't constrained to the consumer market. Great leaps of activity are occurring in the commercial space with semi-trucks, delivery vans, school buses, and other vehicles. Amazon recently announced that they are purchasing 1,800 electric delivery vans from Mercedes-Benz. This follows their gigantic one-hundred-thousand-unit order from Rivian that was announced in late 2019. The US Postal Service is considering bids to start replacing its aging fleet of delivery vehicles. That could be a purchase of as many as 186,000 trucks. Industry stalwarts like GM and companies you have never heard of (e.g., Bollinger, Chanje, and Workhorse) are launching into production. Especially for start-and-stop delivery trucks that return to a garage every day, electric vehicles are a great choice. The sound you don't hear on the street outside your house is the new generation of electric delivery trucks.

## ACCELERATING INNOVATION

As is true for many emerging technologies, vehicle electrification is experiencing rapid innovation. Of the many examples, one is described in Brynjolfsson and McAfee's excellent book, *The Second Machine Age: Work, Progress, and Prosperity in a Time of Brilliant Technologies*. The example described below, although not focused on EVs, shows how quickly digital vehicle control is progressing.

In 2002, the US government's Defense Advanced Research Projects Agency (DARPA) announced its first Grand Challenge. They would award a $1 million prize to any qualifying team that could design and demonstrate an autonomous vehicle that could complete a 142-mile course laid out through California's Mojave Desert. Vehicles could be powered with any drive technology. In March of 2004, fifteen qualifying teams competed in the event.

The results were very disappointing. Two vehicles were unable to start, and one rolled over in the starting area. After three hours, only four cars were still in the competition. A car from Carnegie Mellon University performed the best by covering 7.4 miles before crashing after coming off a switchback. DARPA didn't award the prize money. Popular Science described the event as the "DARPA's Debacle in the Desert." Several technology experts stated that autonomous driving is extremely complex and that we probably would not see autonomous vehicles for another twenty to twenty-five years.

However, six years later in October 2010, Google announced that they had successfully operated completely autonomous vehicles on American roads and highways. By the summer of 2012, Google's Chauffeur project had logged over two hundred thousand miles with no human intervention and only two accidents. Obviously, the experts had overestimated the difficulties and time it would take for the technology to improve.

The pundits got it wrong for two reasons. They failed to see that our rate of innovation is now sometimes faster than we can comprehend. Also, they were unaware of the full spectrum of development taking place, including proprietary development. EV innovation is exhibiting the same acceleration.

EV battery development is steeply climbing the technology innovation curve. Companies see the rapidly expanding battery market for vehicles and homes and are investing heavily in research. This will result in batteries holding more energy and costing less to manufacture.

Brynjolfsson and McAfee offer another insight. Every technology, from steam engines to sewing machines to electric vehicles, experiences a lag in adoption compared to development. People don't jump on the new technology bandwagon immediately. They want to see how the new technology holds up. Adoption typically follows a succession from innovators, to early adopters, to early majority, to late majority, to those who lag behind. EV adoption has passed both the innovator and early-adopters' stages and is now entering the early-majority stage. In 2021, watch for a barrage of news articles on the business page about the expansion of electric car sales as the market goes mainstream.

## GOVERNMENT MANDATES

In many places around the world, people are embracing electric vehicle technology. Governments are doing the same. Some governments are mandating a switch to EVs.

In India, Prime Minister Narendra Modi, who was reelected by a wide margin in 2019, is planning to require all two-wheeled motorized vehicles to be electric by 2026. Of some 250 million registered vehicles, two-wheelers—including mopeds and motorcycles—dominate India's transportation market with about 190 million units. To support this initiative, India's giant conglomerate the Tata Group pledged to build three hundred rapid-charge stations in five major Indian cities.

According to Bloomberg News, China is considering a goal of having 60 percent of all automobiles sold in the country be electric. They refer to these as "new energy vehicles." The category includes pure electric, plug-in hybrids, and fuel-cell vehicles. Through a complicated crediting formula, the Chinese government now requires all automakers, domestic and foreign, to produce a certain percentage of electric vehicles. This mandate is expected to get stricter over time, perhaps rising to as much as 7 percent by 2025.

These Chinese mandates have global implications. Foreign car companies have made major investments in China and are committed to protecting that investment. For example, Volkswagen sells about 40 percent of its global production in China. Accordingly, Volkswagen has dedicated significant resources to the development of EVs.

Even more aligned with the Chinese mandate is Volvo Cars. Volvo will not develop any more new internal-combustion-engine vehicles. It plans to launch five battery electric vehicles between 2019 and 2021. As of 2010, Volvo is owned by Geely Holding Group, a Chinese automotive company. Geely has been developing electric cars for more than a decade.

The UK has set a national goal of eliminating carbon emission by 2050. About a third of greenhouse gas emissions in the UK come from transportation, so they plan to ban petrol and diesel cars in 2035. The plan is expected to include hybrid and plug-in hybrid vehicles. The expectation is that sales will shift drastically to EVs.

California is the largest passenger car market in the United States. In September 2020, California Governor Gavin Newsom signed an executive order that bans the sale of new gasoline powered passenger cars in the state starting in the year 2035. California is following the lead of 15 countries that have mandated similar bans on the sale of new gas-powered vehicles. The governor said that the regulations will be implemented by the California Air Resources Board (CARB). CARB will develop the regulations. The regulations will have some caveats. Gasoline-powered vehicles will still be allowed on the roads after 2035. It will not pertain to the sale of used gas-powered vehicles. Commercial vehicles will be treated differently. It will not pertain to the sale of new medium-duty and new heavy-duty vehicles until the year 2045.

## MODERNIZED POWER GRID AND RENEWABLE ENERGY

Powering electric cars requires both the generation and distribution of electric energy. Throughout the US, coal has been the leading source of energy for electric power generation. Recently that has changed.

Electric energy generation by renewable sources has doubled since 2008. Almost 90 percent of the increase in renewables came from wind- and solar-power generation. Both have much less environmental impact than coal, oil, or natural gas. Coal-fired generating plants are being closed as the cost of renewables has dropped below the cost of coal generation.

Wind generation increased due to taller and more efficient wind turbines. Now the US is following other countries in locating wind turbines offshore. As of 2016, wind provided 8 percent of US electric generation.

Around the world, some 3,500 hydroelectric dams are planned or are being built. However, in the US, hydro generation is at a standstill. Few dams are being built in the US, and some are being removed. In 2018, eighty-two dams were removed. Thus, the share of electric energy provided by hydropower in the US will not increase.

Dam removal is driven by the many environmental benefits it provides, such as helping to increase fish populations by opening upriver spawning grounds and allowing rich sediments to move downstream where they can be used by forests and farmland. Removal can also be driven by financial benefits. Because many US dams are old, it can be less expensive to remove them than repair them.

Electricity generated by solar photovoltaic cells has risen quickly in the US. In 2018, about 4 percent of the total electric energy generated came from solar panels. Two-thirds of that supply was from rooftops and other small plants.

Projecting the future is an iffy proposition, but looking ahead suggests that the future is bright for renewables. The *Motley Fool* combined data sources to conservatively calculate that wind and solar sources will supply almost 50 percent of the total US electricity supply by 2030. About 3 percent of the total electricity generation is expected to come from offshore installations, up from almost zero today. For solar, more than 5 percent of total generation could come from small-scale solar installations like those on residential rooftops, which are becoming cheaper and more prevalent. Adding in the contributions of nuclear power plants could bring the total share of US electricity generated by "zero-carbon" sources up from 40 percent, where it is today, to almost 70 percent in 2030. Nuclear is by no means ideal, but it is serving to bridge the gap to a zero-carbon future. The remaining 30 percent would most likely be generated by lower-carbon natural gas.

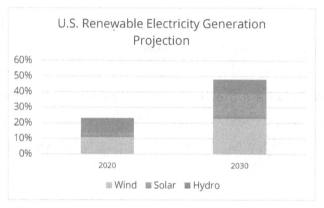

This chart shows the projected change in the percent of electricity generated by segments of renewable energy.

EVs will play a key role in modernizing the US power grid through a concept called "vehicle-to-grid" (V2G). V2G is an enhanced-power-er-grid concept where electric vehicles become integrated into the grid. EVs will communicate with the grid to provide two benefits.

One is smart charging. EV owners who can charge their cars whenever they want will respond to rate changes charged by utilities. Since most cars sit unused 95 percent of the time, they can be charged at any time of the day, and owners will take advantage of changes in the rate utilities charge.

Utilities sell electric power like any commodity. When demand is high, they will charge more. To optimize the power load, utilities will lower rates at off-peak times to encourage charging at these times. This shifting of demand helps utilities even the drain on their system.

The second benefit is that EVs will be connected to the grid as a temporary battery. Having many thousands of EV batteries connected to the grid will allow utilities to draw energy briefly from the cars and use it where it is needed. EV battery charging resumes when the short spike in demand has reduced. As intermittent power sources such as wind and solar generation provide a larger share of electric power, having EVs store and return power as clouds pass and winds fluctuate smooths out the supply.

Making V2G a reality will take time to design, standardize, and deploy. Work on V2G standards are already underway in some forms, such as the CHAdeMO charge system described above.

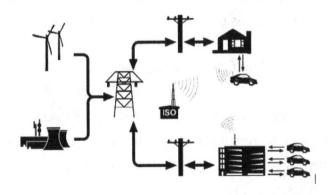

Vehicle-to-Grid Architecture: This diagram shows a typical V2G architecture. Power is generated at power plants and wind farms and carried to consumers by the electric grid. EVs are used to store energy generated by wind and solar during the day and then return it to the grid when needed at night.

## E<small>LECTRIC</small> M<small>OTORCYCLES</small>

Raising eyebrows, Harley Davidson launched its first electric motorcycle in 2019. Called the LiveWire, it has a 105-horsepower motor with a 15.5 kWh battery for 105 miles of range. Its performance, power, and design are very impressive.

The LiveWire has a 3.1-second zero to sixty time, which is as fast as "superbikes" like the 2020 BMW S 1000 RR. This puts it at parity with its four-wheeled EV cousins that can outperform gas-powered "supercars."

As motorcycles go, the LiveWire is expensive, with a $29,799 price tag. Harley Davidson seems to be following Tesla's strategy of leading with a premium-priced vehicle that clearly demonstrates the potential of electrification. It is pretty clear that Harley Davidson built the LiveWire to demonstrate their commitment to electric motorcycles and to get their market excited about their new electric bikes that are sure to follow.

## T<small>HE</small> C<small>OMMERCIAL</small> S<small>EGMENT</small>

Commercial fleet owners are always concerned with both the price of fuel and with the pollution their vehicles emit. Carbon-neutral initiatives are being taken more seriously, which is driving enthusiasm for EVs.

In September 2019, Amazon announced that it ordered one hundred thousand fully electric delivery vans from Rivian Automotive LLC, based in Michigan. The first ten thousand vans are expected to be on the road by 2022. The agreement is esti-mated to cost $4 billion, and it will double the number of electric delivery vans in the world. In addition to helping Amazon reach its goal of becoming carbon neutral by 2040, the e-vans reduce Amazon's fuel costs. Amazon is so sensitive to fuel costs that it cited it as a reason for raising the price of its Prime membership.

Other large fleet owners are just as concerned about fuel costs as Amazon. For UPS, fuel expenses grew by $1.3 billion from 2016 to 2018. We have to wonder when they and other fleet owners will start making the switch to EVs.

Heavy-duty trucking is also going electric. The world's largest truck manufacturer, Daimler Trucks North America (DTNA), has fully embraced EVs. They announced several EV versions of their dominant product line, the Freightliner eCascadia Class 8 (heavy duty) semi-truck, the eM2 medium-duty truck, and the Saf-T-Liner C2 Thomas Built school bus.

Volvo Trucks, the world's second-largest truck manufacturer, expects to start selling an all-electric Class 8 regional hauler, dubbed the EVNR, at the end of 2020. Volvo is also in collabora-tion with the California Air Resources Board and fourteen other organizations on a project called Volvo LIGHTS. The goal is to develop charging and workflow innovations that will ensure the commercial success of battery electric trucks.

In November 2017, Tesla sent shock waves through the commer-cial trucking industry when it unveiled its Tesla Semi. As with its other vehicles, Tesla completely redesigned the category of tractors. So far, Tesla has announced two trucks with ranges of three hundred and six hundred miles. This range is certainly adequate for the regional delivery market.

One of the big challenges facing the trucking industry is driver shortages. Electric trucks will make it easier to recruit and train drivers because they are much simpler to drive than diesel-power trucks as there is no complicated gear shifting to learn.

The switch from fossil-fuel-powered internal-combustion vehicles to EVs is occurring in transit buses and school buses. Thomas Built Buses (TBB), a division of DTNA, is one leader. TBB partnered with a Proterra, a leader in EV technology solutions for heavy-duty applications, to develop an all-electric school bus called the Saf-T-Liner C2 Jouley. School buses are an ideal EV application given their range profile and the fact that they return to the same depot where they can be recharged every day.

Bloomberg New Energy Finance projects that (EVs) will reach 10 percent of global passenger vehicle sales in 2025. That percentage will rise to 28 percent by 2030 and 58 percent by 2040. The future looks very bright for EVs, and the future starts now in 2021.

# TECHNICAL DEFINITIONS AND EXPLAINERS

If you are used to gas-powered cars, the world of electric vehicles can seem like a parallel universe with its own language. Here is a summary of terms and equivalencies.

| | |
|---|---|
| AMP | An ampere is a way to measure electricity. It is defined as the amount of charge, or current, flowing through the circuit over a period of time. An ampere, or amp, is defined as one Coulomb of charge per second passing through a point in a circuit. |
| BEV | Battery Electric Vehicle, also referred to as "pure EVs" or EVs. These cars require no gasoline and are powered 100 percent by rechargeable batteries. Their main components are batteries, one or more motors, and a motor control system that manages torque, traction slip, and regenerative braking. |
| CAFE | Corporate Average Fuel Economy is the United States regulation first enacted in 1975 to improve the average fuel economy of cars, light-duty trucks, vans, and SUVs. CAFE standards are set by the NHTSA. |

| | |
|---|---|
| DC-to-DC Converter | The auxiliary systems in cars run on electricity. Electric cars have lots of electric power stored in the main or traction batteries, but it is not at the voltage the auxiliary systems need. The DC-DC Converter takes the high voltage from the traction battery and supplies lower voltages to the car's other systems. |
| Drag Coefficient (Cd) | The drag coefficient of an automobile is a measure of how efficiently it passes through the surrounding air. Aerodynamic drag increases with the square of speed, making it critically important at higher speeds. Reducing the drag coefficient of an EV will increase its range. Typical automobiles have a drag coefficient of 0.25 to 0.3. Vehicles with a blunter shape like SUVs typically have a drag coefficient of 0.35 to 0.45. |
| EPA | Environmental Protection Agency. A US federal agency that conducts environmental assessment, research, and education. It has the responsibility of maintaining and enforcing national standards under a variety of environmental laws, in consultation with state, tribal, and local governments. |
| Euro NCAP | European New Car Assessment Program. This is a voluntary European car safety performance assessment program. It is based in Leuven, Belgium, and was formed in 1996. It is backed by the European Union. |
| FCEV | Fuel-Cell Electric Vehicle, also referred to as hydrogen vehicles. FCEVs use hydrogen as the main source of power. The hydrogen is fed into a fuel cell that converts hydrogen to electricity, with water as a byproduct. That power is then used to deliver a steady current to a battery pack. The batteries power the motor and other systems. |

| | |
|---|---|
| HEV | Hybrid Electric Vehicle. These vehicles are essentially the combination of an EV and an ICE vehicle. They have both drive systems, with all of the associated complexity and cost. An example is the Toyota Prius. HEVs started to gain popularity in 2005 and peaked around 2012. As BEVs' ranges have improved, they have steadily taken market share from HEVs. |
| ICE | Internal-Combustion Engine. This acronym describes any vehicle that runs on fossil fuels, including gasoline and diesel. |
| Inverter | The driving or traction motors in an EV use alternating current or AC. The batteries storing energy in an EV store it as direct current or DC. To convert from DC to AC requires an inverter—sometimes called a "traction inverter." This electronic device takes the steady DC current from the batteries, inverts it into alternating current, and parcels it out to the motors at the rate they require. An electronic controller tells the inverter how much power is required. It takes the input from the accelerator your foot is pushing on and directs the inverter to release the required electric power. |
| Kilowatt (kW) | A measurement of electrical power, usually abbreviated as "kW." When used to express an electric motor's maximum output, this is roughly equivalent to 1.34 horsepower. |
| Kilowatt-Hour (kWh) | Kilowatt-hour is a measure of electric energy that is equivalent to the energy expended in one hour by one thousand watts of power. EV battery capacity is typically expressed in terms of kWh. |
| Level 1 Charging | Level 1 is the slowest way to charge an EV. It uses a standard 110-volt wall outlet. Level 1 charging typically adds about four miles of range per hour (RPH). Depending on the model of EV it can take between eight and twenty-four hours to recharge the battery. |

| | |
|---|---|
| Level 2 Charging | Level 2 charging is typically what people install in their homes. It requires a 240-volt electric circuit like those used for large electric appliances like dryers or stoves. Level 2 charging adds about twenty-five miles of range per hour. You can have a Level 2 charger installed by a professional electrician at home. |
| Level 3 Charging | Level 3 is the fastest way to recharge an EV battery. It is also called DC fast charging. Level 3 requires a 480-volt electric circuit that is typically only found in commercially zoned areas. It can usually recharge a battery up to 80 percent in less than a half hour. Level 3 equipment is not compatible with all vehicles. For example, all Teslas and the Nissan LEAF can accept a Level 3 charge, but the Chevy Volt cannot. There is currently no industry standard for this level of charging. They are being deployed across the United States in public or commercial settings, with Tesla being the only brand with a coast-to-coast infrastructure already installed. |
| MPGe | Miles Per Gallon equivalent. This is an energy efficiency metric that was introduced by the Environmental Protection Agency in 2010 to compare the amount of energy consumed by alternative fuel vehicles to that of traditional gas-powered cars. |
| NHTSA | The National Highway Traffic Safety Administration is a United States federal government agency charged with keeping people safe on America's roadways. This includes writing and enforcing Federal Motor Vehicle Safety Standards. The NHTSA performs standardized vehicle safety tests, including crash tests, and provides results in an easy-to-understand five-star rating that helps consumers make smart decisions about safety when purchasing a vehicle. |

| | |
|---|---|
| PHEV | Plug-In Hybrid Electric Vehicle. These are hybrid electric vehicles with larger batteries that can be plugged in like those in an EV. The larger battery gives these cars more range on electric drive than a standard hybrid vehicle, so it relies less on the gasoline motor. |
| Power Band | The range of RPM around peak power output. Electric motors usually have a flat power band, meaning that they deliver maximum torque the moment they start turning. Internal-combustion engines must reach a certain RPM before they reach their power band. |
| Regenerative Braking | A process used in EVs (and some hybrid electric vehicles) that recovers energy otherwise lost during deceleration and braking and sends it back to the battery pack to help maintain a charge. Some EVs, like Teslas and the Nissan LEAF, maximize the regenerative braking effect to slow the vehicle and even bring it to a stop with little assistance from the traditional brakes. This is commonly called one-pedal driving. Regenerative braking is why EVs get extraordinary brake life, with most not needing brake pad replacement until over 150,000 miles. |
| REHEV | Range-Extended Hybrid Electric Vehicles. A REHEV is a BEV with a small gasoline engine that powers a generator to recharge the batteries. Examples are the Chevy Volt and the BMW i3 REX. The difference between a REHEV and a HEV is that the REHEV's gasoline engine isn't connected to the drivetrain. |
| REX | Range-Extended Electric Vehicle. See REHEV. |
| RPM | Revolutions Per Minute. |
| SOC | State of Charge. Typically refers to the meter on an EV's instrument panel that displays the battery's current level of charge. |

| | |
|---|---|
| Specific Energy | The amount of energy a battery can store divided by its weight. It is sometimes casually referred to as energy density. For the technical folks out there, it is joules per kilogram. |
| Torque | Described first by Archimedes, torque is the rotational force that causes a shaft to spin. It is the rotational equivalent of linear force. One advantage of EVs is that electric motors deliver 100 percent of their available torque instantaneously. This enables their fast launches and superior passing ability. |
| V2G | Vehicle-to-grid (also referred to as vehicle-grid-integration, VTI) is an enhanced power-grid concept in which electric vehicles become integrated with the grid. EVs will communicate with the grid to enable two main benefits. EVs will be able to adjust their charge rate to minimize load on the electrical grid. Also, they will be able to store and then return electricity to the grid that has been generated by renewable sources like solar and wind. This is important because renewable power sources fluctuate depending on time of day and weather. |
| Watt (W) | Named after the Scottish inventor James Watt, the Watt is used to quantify the rate of energy transfer or power. It is defined as one joule of work performed per second. An equivalent is the power dissipated in an electrical conductor carrying one ampere current at one volt. |
| ZEV | Zero Emissions Vehicle. A vehicle that has no tailpipe emissions. All BEVs, or pure electric vehicles, are classified as ZEV. |

# ABOUT THE AUTHORS

The authors are an engineer who drives an electric car and is a serious car buff, and a scientist and science educator who has published 34 books.

Photo by John Gallagher www.bygallagher.com

## Chris Johnston

Chris Johnston has decades of product management experience in telematics, mobile computing and wireless communications including positions at Trimble Navigation, AT&T, Honeywell and a couple of Silicon Valley startups. He also spent a year in India setting up an Internet-of-things practice for a major Indian corporation. Mr. Johnston has a B.S. in electrical engineering from Purdue University and an MBA from Loyola University of Chicago. Chris lives in Washington State with his wife and two kids. When not working, he enjoys open water swimming, cycling and flying (as a private pilot).

## Ed Sobey

Ed Sobey holds a PhD in science and teaches for Semester at Sea. He also lectures at sea for passengers on several cruise lines and has traveled the equivalent of ten times around the world at sea.

The Fulbright Commission has awarded Ed two grants for training science teachers in foreign countries. To date he has trained teachers in more than 30 countries. He is a former naval officer and has directed five science centers, published 34 books, and hosted two television series on science and technology.

Ed is a Fellow of The Explorers Club and has participated in two dozen scientific expeditions. He has conducted ocean research in winter in Antarctica; sailed across the Pacific Ocean in a small sail-boat, and recorded whale sounds from an ocean kayak. He organizes and leads citizen science expeditions for the nonprofit Northwest Explorers.

# END NOTES

## From Birth through Maturation: A History of Electric Vehicles

Zachary Shahan. "Tesla Model 3 Dominates US Premium-Class Small & Midsize Car Market" *CleanTechnica*, 18 Jan. 2020, https://cleantechnica.com/2020/01/18/tesla-model-3-dominates-us-premium-class-small-midsize-car-market-24-of-2019-sales/. Accessed July 2020.

Fred Lambert. "Tesla Model 3 beats Honda Civic as top-selling car in California" *electrek*, 29 May 2020, https://electrek.co/2020/05/29/tesla-model-3-beats-honda-civic-top-selling-car-california/. Accessed July 2020.

Tom Raftery. "Seven Reasons Why the Internal Combustion Engine Is A Dead Man Walking" *Forbes*, 6 Sept. 2018, https://www.forbes.com/sites/sap/2018/09/06/seven-reasons-why-the-internal-combustion-engine-is-a-dead-man-walking-updated/#3f4338fb603f. Accessed July 2020.

"National Household Travel Survey Daily Travel Quick Facts" *Bureau of Transportation Statistics*, 31 May 2017, U.S. Department of Transportation, https://www.bts.gov/statistical-products/surveys/national-household-travel-survey-daily-travel-quick-facts. Accessed July 2020.

John Voelcker. "2011 Nissan LEAF Electric Car Crosses 150,000 Miles of Commuting" *Green Car Reports*, 28 May 2016, https://www.greencarreports.com/news/1089091_owner-of-100000-mile-nissan-leaf-electric-car-to-be-honored-monday. Accessed July 2020.

Wayne Cunningham. "2011 Nissan Leaf review", *Road Show by CNET*, 6 Dec. 2010, https://www.cnet.com/roadshow/reviews/2011-nissan-leaf-review/. Accessed July 2020.

*www.fueleconomy.gov*, U.S. Department of Energy, https://www.fueleconomy.gov/feg/Find.do?action=sbs&id=30979. Accessed July 2020.

Rob Stumpf. "Americans Cite Range Anxiety, Cost as Largest Barriers for New EV Purchases" *The Drive*, 26 Feb. 2019, https://www.thedrive.com/news/26637/americans-cite-range-anxiety-cost-as-largest-barriers-for-new-ev-purchases-study. Accessed July 2020.

"EV Charging Statistics" *EVAdoption*, 31 Mar. 2019, https://evadoption.com/ev-charging-stations-statistics/#:~:text=As%20of%20December%2031%2C%202017,average%20of%202.75%20stations%2Foutlets.. Accessed July 2020.

"Nissan Announces National Market Roll-Out Plan For Zero-Emission Nissan LEAF" *Nissan Motor Corporation*, 27 July 2010, https://usa.nissannews.com/en-US/releases/nissan-announces-national-market-roll-out-plan-for-zero-emission-nissan-leaf#. Accessed July 2020.

Nigel Burton. A History of Electric Cars. Crowood, 30 June 2013.

## EV Advantages

Argonne National Laboratory. "Overview of the Design, Construction, and Operation of Interstate Liquid Petroleum Pipelines" *U.S. Department of Energy*, Nov. 2007, https://publications.anl.gov/anlpubs/2008/01/60928.pdf. Accessed Aug 2020.

Ignasi Palou-Rivera and Michael Wang. "Estimation of Energy Efficiencies of U.S. Petroleum Refineries" *Center for Transportation Research Argonne National Laboratory*, Dec. 2010, https://publications.anl.gov/anlpubs/2011/01/69026.pdf.  Accessed July 2020.

Stacy Davis, Susan Diegel and Robert Boundy. "Transportation Energy Data Book, Edition 28" *Energy Efficiency and Renewable Energy*, 2009, U.S. Department of Energy, https://info.ornl.gov/sites/publications/files/Pub20096.pdf. Accessed July 2020.

National Research Council. Hidden Costs of Energy: Unpriced Consequences of Energy Production and Use. Washington, DC, The National Academies Press, 2009.

"Greenhouse Gas Emissions from a Typical Passenger Vehicle" *U.S. Environmental Protection Agency*, https://www.epa.gov/green-vehicles/greenhouse-gas-emissions-typical-passenger-ve-hicle#:~:text=typical%20passenger%20vehicle%3F-,A%20typical%20passenger%20vehicle%20emits%20about%20-4.6%20metric%20tons%20of,8%2C887%20grams%20of%20CO2. Accessed July 2020.

"Learn about CFLs" *Energy Star*, https://www.energystar.gov/products/lighting_fans/light_bulbs/learn_about_cfls. Accessed July 2020.

"Learn About LED Lighting" *Energy Star*, https://www.energystar.gov/products/lighting_fans/light_bulbs/learn_about_led_bulbs#led_differences. Accessed July 2020.

"Weekly Retail Gasoline and Diesel Prices" *U.S. Energy Information Administration*, https://www.eia.gov/dnav/pet/pet_pri_gnd_dcus_nus_m.htm. Accessed July 2020.

"Electric Power Monthly" *U.S. Energy Information Administration*, https://www.eia.gov/electricity/monthly/epm_table_grapher.php?t=epmt_5_06_b. Accessed July 2020.

"Brake Repair Prices" *Kelley Blue Book*, https://www.kbb.com/brake-repair/. Accessed July 2020.

John O'Dell. "What Makes a Tesla Special? These 10 Things, for Starters" *nerdwallet*, 20 July 2016, https://www.nerdwallet.com/blog/loans/whats-special-tesla-10/?trk=nw-wire_305_277083_24336. Accessed July 2020.

Tom Raftery. "Seven Reasons Why the Internal Combustion Engine Is A Dead Man Walking" *Forbes*, 6 Sept. 2018, https://www.forbes.com/sites/sap/2018/09/06/seven-reasons-why-the-internal-combustion-engine-is-a-dead-man-walking-updated/#3f4338fb603f. Accessed July 2020.

## EV Myths

"Today in Energy" *U.S. Energy Information Administration*, 19 Mar. 2019, U.S. Energy Information Administration, https://www.eia.gov/todayinenergy/detail.php?id=38752#:~:text=Renewables%20provided%2017.6%25%20of%20electricity,from%20wind%20and%20solar%20generation. Accessed July 2020.

Brian Fung. "Elon Musk's snarky response to a Koch-brothers plan to kill electric cars" *The Washington Post*, 19 Feb. 2016, https://www.washingtonpost.com/news/the-switch/wp/2016/02/19/elon-musks-snarky-response-to-a-koch-brothers-plan-to-kill-electric-cars/. Accessed July 2020.

Marianna Lovo. "Lead Battery Industry Issues New National Recycling Rate Study" *Battery Council International*, 14 Nov. 2019, https://batterycouncil.org/blogpost/1190989/334861/Lead-Battery-Industry-Issues-New-National-Recycling-Rate-Study. Accessed July 2020.

Matteo Muratori. "Impact of uncoordinated plug-in electric vehicle charging on residential power demand" *Nature Research*, 22 Jan 2018, https://www.nature.com/articles/s41560-017-0074-z. Accessed July 2020.

## Electric Vehicle Type Choices

Larry Hall. "What The Heck Is A 'Compliance Car'?" *ThoughtCo*, 7 Feb. 2019, https://www.thoughtco.com/what-is-a-compliance-car-85648#:~:text=Thus%2C%20the%20Chevrolet%20Spark%20EV,selling%20cars%20in%20the%20state.. Accessed July 2020.

## EV Buying Guide

"Ratings" *National Highway Traffic Safety Administration*, United States Department of Transportation, https://www.nhtsa.gov/ratings. Accessed July 2020.

"Ratings & Rewards" *Euro NCAP*, https://www.euroncap.com/en/ratings-rewards/. Accessed July 2020.

Bart Demandt. "Jaguar I-PACE U.S. Sales Figures" *Carsalesbase*, https://carsalesbase.com/us-jaguar-i-pace/. Accessed July 2020.

"Polestar announces new management team" Polestar, 21 June 2017, https://www.polestar.com/global/press/press-release/polestar-announces-new-management-team. Accessed July 2020.

Elon Musk. "The Secret Tesla Motors Master Plan (just between you and me)" *Tesla*, 2 Aug. 2006, https://www.tesla.com/blog/secret-tesla-motors-master-plan-just-between-you-and-me#:~:text=So%2C%20in%20short%2C%20the%20master,emission%20electric%20power%20generation%20options. Accessed July 2020.

## Owning an EV

"How much can you save on your Los Angeles Department of Water and Power (LADWP) electric payment by swapping to a cheaper rate plan and/or installing solar?" *cutmybill*, Los Angeles Department of Water & Power, https://cutmybill.com/best-ladwp-electric-rate-plans. Accessed July 2020.

"EV Rebates" *Tucson Electric Power*, Los Angeles Department of Water & Power, https://www.tep.com/ev-rebates/. Accessed July 2020.

## Future

Erik Brynjolfsson and Andrew McAfee. The Second Machine Age: Work, Progress, and Prosperity in a Time of Brilliant Technologies. Norton & Company, 2014.

Scott Carpenter. "India's Plan To Turn 200 Million Vehicles Electric In Six Years" *Forbes*, 5 Dec. 2019, https://www.forbes.com/sites/scottcarpenter/2019/12/05/can-india-turn-nearly-200-million-vehicles-electric-in-six-years/#3c5e05bd15db. Accessed July 2020.

Jack Barkenbus. "The electric vehicle revolution will come from China, not the US" *The Conversation*, 14 May 2019, https://theconversation.com/the-electric-vehicle-revolution-will-come-from-china-not-the-us-116102#:~:text=The%20Chinese%20government%20now%20requires,their%20sales%20electric%20by%202025. Accessed July 2020.

Ying Tian and Steven Yang. "China Mulls Goal of 60% of Auto Sales to be electric by 2035" *Bloomberg*, 6 Sept. 2019, https://www.bloomberg.com/news/articles/2019-09-06/china-mulls-target-for-60-of-auto-sales-to-be-electric-by-2035?utm_source=twitter&cmpid=socialflow-twitter-business&utm_medium=social&utm_campaign=socialflow-organic&utm_content=business. Accessed July 2020.

"Volvo goes electric across the board" *BBC News*, 5 July 2017, https://www.bbc.com/news/business-40505671. Accessed July 2020.

"How will the petrol and diesel car ban work?" *BBC News*, 4 Feb. 2020, https://www.bbc.com/news/uk-40726868. Accessed July 2020.

Maxx Chatsko. "How Much U.S. Electricity Will Come From Renewables in 2030?" *The Motley Fool*, 21 Oct. 2019, https://www.fool.com/investing/2019/10/21/how-much-us-electricity-will-come-from-renewables.aspx. Accessed July 2020.

Trefis Team. "How Big Is Purchased Transportation Cost For UPS?" *Forbes*, 23 Dec. 2019, https://www.forbes.com/sites/greatspeculations/2019/12/23/how-big-is-purchased-transportation-cost-for-ups/#31de4bee6299. Accessed July 2020.

Andrew Hawkins. "Amazon will order 100,000 electric delivery vans from EV startup Rivian" *The Verge*, 19 Sept. 2019, https://www.theverge.com/2019/9/19/20873947/amazon-electric-delivery-van-rivian-jeff-bezos-order. Accessed July 2020.

# PHOTO ATTRIBUTION

Photo description: 2008 Tesla Roadster
- Photo Title: Roadster 2.5 windmills trimmed.jpg
- Name of the creator: Tesla Motors Inc.
- This photograph is copyrighted
- License notice: The copyright holder of this work allows anyone to use it for any purpose including unrestricted redistribution, commercial use, and modification
- Link to the material: https://commons.wikimedia.org/wiki/File:Roadster_2.5_windmills_trimmed.jpg

Photo description: 2011 Nissan LEAF
- Photo Title: 2011 Nissan LEAF
- Name of the creator: Tennen-Gas
- This photograph is copyrighted
- License notice: Creative Commons Attribution-Share Alike 3.0 Unported license
- Link to the material: https://commons.wikimedia.org/wiki/File:Nissan_Leaf_001.JPG

Photo description: Tesla Model S
- Photo Title: Tesla Model S Indoors trimmed.jpg
- Name of the creator: Mariordo (Mario R. Duran Ortiz)
- This photograph is copyrighted
- License notice: Creative Commons Attribution 2.0 Generic license

- Link to the material: https://commons.wikimedia.org/wiki/ File:Tesla_Model_S_Indoors_trimmed.jpg

Photo description: Jaguar I-PACE
- Photo Title: Jaguar I-Pace- Mortefontaine 01.jpg
- Name of the creator: Y.Leclercq
- This photograph is copyrighted
- License notice: Creative Commons Attribution-Share Alike 4.0 International license.
- Link to the material: https://commons.wikimedia.org/wiki/File:- Jaguar_I-Pace-_Mortefontaine_01.jpg

Photo description: General Motors EV1
- Photo Title: EV1A014 (1) cropped.jpg
- Name of the creator: RightBrainPhotography (Rick Rowen)
- This photograph is copyrighted
- License notice: Creative Commons Attribution-Share Alike 2.0 Generic license.
- Link to the material: https://commons.wikimedia.org/wiki/ File:EV1A014_(1)_cropped.jpg

Photo description: Toyota RAV4 EV
- Photo Title: Toyota RAV4 EV WAS 2012 0821.jpg
- Name of the creator: Mariordo - Mario Roberto Durán Ortiz
- This photograph is copyrighted
- License notice: Creative Commons Attribution-Share Alike 3.0 Unported license.
- Link to the material: https://commons.wikimedia.org/wiki/ File:Toyota_RAV4_EV_WAS_2012_0821.jpg

Photo description: BMW i3
- Photo Title: BMW-i3-Side.JPG
- Name of the creator: RudolfSimon
- This photograph is copyrighted
- License notice: Creative Commons Attribution-Share Alike 3.0 Unported license.
- Link to the material: https://commons.wikimedia.org/wiki/File:B- MW-i3-Side.JPG

Photo description: Gustave Trouve riding three-wheeled electric car 1881
- Photo Title: Capture d'écran 2016-10-14 à 21.26.28.png
- Name of the creator: Jacques CATTELIN
- This photograph is copyrighted

- License notice: Creative Commons Attribution-Share Alike 4.0 International license
- Link to the material: https://commons.wikimedia.org/w/index.php?curid=52267675

Photo description: Pump Jack at the Lost Hills Oil Field In Central California

- Photo Title: Pump Jack at the Lost Hills Oil Field In Central California.jpg
- Name of the creator: Richard Masoner
- This photograph is copyrighted
- License notice: Creative Commons Attribution-Share Alike 2.0 Generic license
- Link to the material: https://commons.wikimedia.org/wiki/File:Pump_Jack_at_the_Lost_Hills_Oil_Field_In_Central_California.jpg

Photo description: Mazda RX-8 Under Hood

- Photo Title: Mazda rx-8 under the hood.jpg
- Name of the creator: Neil de Carteret
- This photograph is copyrighted
- License notice: Creative Commons Attribution-Share Alike 3.0 Unported license.
- Link to the material: https://commons.wikimedia.org/wiki/File:Mazda_rx-8_under_the_hood.jpg

Photo description: Audi i3 e-Tron

- Photo Title: Audi A3 e-tron (14646466253).jpg
- Name of the creator: Robert Basic from Germany
- This photograph is copyrighted
- License notice: Creative Commons Attribution-Share Alike 2.0 Generic license.
- Link to the material: https://commons.wikimedia.org/wiki/File:Audi_A3_e-tron_(14646466253).jpg
- Modification: isolated image from background.

Photo description: BMW i3

- Photo Title: BMW-i3-Side.JPG
- Name of the creator: RudolfSimon
- This photograph is copyrighted
- License notice: Creative Commons Attribution-Share Alike 3.0 Unported license.
- Link to the material: https://commons.wikimedia.org/wiki/File:B-MW-i3-Side.JPG

- Modification: isolated image from background.

Photo description: Chevrolet Bolt
- Photo Title: 2019 Chevrolet Bolt EV - April 2019 (2898).jpg
- Name of the creator: Gregory Varnum
- This photograph is copyrighted
- License notice: Creative Commons Attribution-Share Alike 4.0 International license.
- Link to the material: https://commons.wikimedia.org/wiki/File:2019_Chevrolet_Bolt_EV_-_April_2019_(2898).jpg
- Modification: isolated image from background.

Photo description: Ford Mach-e
- Photo Title: Ford Mustang Mach-E GT.jpg
- Name of the creator: Automotive Rhythms
- This photograph is copyrighted
- License notice: Creative Commons Attribution-Share Alike 4.0 International license
- Link to the material: https://commons.wikimedia.org/wiki/File:-Ford_Mustang_Mach-E_GT.jpg
- Modification: isolated image from background.

Photo description: Hyundai Ioniq Electric
- Photo Title: Hyundai Ioniq Electric (12).JPG
- Name of the creator: Pablo Montoya
- This photograph is copyrighted
- License notice: Creative Commons Attribution-Share Alike 4.0 International license
- Link to the material: https://commons.wikimedia.org/wiki/File:Hyundai_Ioniq_Electric_(12).JPG
- Modification: isolated image from background.

Photo description: Hyundai Kona Electric
- Photo Title: Hyundai Kona Electric, Geneva International Motor Show 2018
- Name of the creator: Matti Blume
- This photograph is copyrighted
- License notice: Creative Commons Attribution-Share Alike 4.0 International license
- Link to the material: https://commons.wikimedia.org/wiki/File:-Geneva_International_Motor_Show_2018,_Le_Grand-Saconnex_(1X7A1439).jpg
- Modification: isolated image from background.

Photo description: KIA Niro EV
- Photo Title: Kia E-Niro exposée lors du mondial de l'automobile de Paris 2018
- Name of the creator: Thesupermat
- This photograph is copyrighted
- License notice: Creative Commons Attribution-Share Alike 4.0 International license
- Link to the material: https://commons.wikimedia.org/wiki/File:Kia_E-Niro_-_Mondial_de_l%27Automobile_de_Paris_2018_-_001.jpg
- Modification: isolated image from background.

Photo description: Lordstown Endurance
- Photo Title: Vice President Pence in Ohio (50058668927).jpg
- Name of the creator: The White House from Washington, DC
- This photograph is in the public domain
- Link to the material: https://upload.wikimedia.org/wikipedia/commons/4/4d/Vice_President_Pence_in_Ohio_%2850058668927%29.jpg
- Modification: isolated image from background.

Photo description: Lucid Air
- Photo Title: Lucid Air Rendering.svg
- Name of the creator: Jzh2074
- This photograph is copyrighted
- License notice: Creative Commons Attribution-Share Alike 4.0 International license
- Link to the material: https://upload.wikimedia.org/wikipedia/commons/a/ad/Lucid_Air_Rendering.svg

Photo description: Mini Cooper Electric
- Photo Title: Mini Cooper SE Electric (48804801433).jpg
- Name of the creator: Rutger van der Maar from Leiden, The Netherlands
- This photograph is copyrighted
- License notice: Creative Commons Attribution 2.0 Generic license
- Link to the material: https://commons.wikimedia.org/wiki/File:Mini_Cooper_SE_Electric_(48804801433).jpg
- Modification: isolated image from background.

Photo description: Nissan Ariya
- Photo Title: Nissan Ariya Concept.jpg
- Name of the creator: TTTNIS

- This photograph is copyrighted
- License notice: Creative Commons CC0 1.0 Universal Public Domain Dedication
- Link to the material: https://commons.wikimedia.org/wiki/File:Nissan_Ariya_Concept.jpg
- Modification: isolated image from background.

Photo description: Nissan Leaf 2018
- Photo Title: Nissan Leaf 2018 (31874639158).jpg
- Name of the creator: Kārlis Dambrāns from Latvia
- This photograph is copyrighted
- License notice: Creative Commons Attribution 2.0 Generic license
- Link to the material: https://commons.wikimedia.org/wiki/File:Nissan_Leaf_2018_(31874639158).jpg
- Modification: isolated image from background.

Photo description: Polestar 2
- Photo Title: Polestar 2 Genf 2019 1Y7A6000.jpg
- Name of the creator: Alexander Migl
- This photograph is copyrighted
- License notice: Creative Commons Attribution-Share Alike 4.0 International license
- Link to the material: https://commons.wikimedia.org/wiki/File:Polestar_2_Genf_2019_1Y7A6000.jpg
- Modification: isolated image from background.

Photo description: Porsche Taycan
- Photo Title: Porsche Taycan at IAA 2019 IMG 0249.jpg
- Name of the creator: Alexander Migl
- This photograph is copyrighted
- License notice: Creative Commons Attribution-Share Alike 4.0 International license
- Link to the material: https://commons.wikimedia.org/wiki/File:Porsche_Taycan_at_IAA_2019_IMG_0249.jpg
- Modification: isolated image from background.

Photo description: Rivian R1T
- Photo Title: Debut of the Rivian R1T pickup at the 2018 Los Angeles Auto Show
- Name of the creator: Richard Truesdell
- This photograph is copyrighted
- License notice: Creative Commons Attribution-Share Alike 4.0

International license
- Link to the material: https://commons.wikimedia.org/wiki/ File:Debut_of_the_Rivian_R1T_pickup_at_the_2018_Los_Angeles_ Auto_Show,_November_27,_2018.jpg
- Modification: isolated image from background.

Photo description: Rivian R1S
- Photo Title: Debut of the Rivian R1S SUV at the 2018 Los Angeles Auto Show
- Name of the creator: Richard Truesdell
- This photograph is copyrighted
- License notice: Creative Commons Attribution-Share Alike 4.0 International license
- Link to the material: https://commons.wikimedia.org/wiki/ File:Debut_of_the_Rivian_R1S_SUV_at_the_2018_Los_Angeles_ Auto_Show,_November_27,_2018.jpg
- Modification: isolated image from background.

Photo description: Tesla Model X
- Photo Title: Tesla Model X vin0002 trimmed.jpg
- Name of the creator: Steve Jurvetson
- This photograph is copyrighted
- License notice: Creative Commons Attribution 2.0 Generic license
- Link to the material: https://commons.wikimedia.org/wiki/ File:Tesla_Model_X_vin0002_trimmed.jpg
- Modification: isolated image from background.

Photo description: Tesla Model 3
- Photo Title: TeslaModel3-kobe-japan.jpg
- Name of the creator: Raneko2
- This photograph is copyrighted
- License notice: Creative Commons Attribution-Share Alike 4.0 International license
- Link to the material: https://commons.wikimedia.org/wiki/ File:TeslaModel3-kobe-japan.jpg
- Modification: isolated image from background.

Photo description: Tesla Model Y
- Photo Title: 2020 Tesla Model Y, front 8.1.20.jpg
- Name of the creator: Kevauto
- This photograph is copyrighted
- License notice: Creative Commons Attribution-Share Alike 4.0

International license
- Link to the material: https://commons.wikimedia.org/wiki/File:2020_Tesla_Model_Y,_front_8.1.20.jpg
- Modification: isolated image from background.

Photo description: Tesla Roadster 2.0
- Photo Title: Tesla Roadster 2.0 (47619421652).jpg
- Name of the creator: Steve Jurvetson from Menlo Park, USA
- This photograph is copyrighted
- License notice: Creative Commons Attribution 2.0 Generic license
- Link to the material: https://commons.wikimedia.org/wiki/File:Tesla_Roadster_2.0_(47619421652).jpg
- Modification: isolated image from background.

Photo description: Tesla Cybertruck
- Photo Title: Tesla Cybertruck outside unveil modified by Smnt.jpg
- Name of the creator:
- This photograph is copyrighted
- License notice: Creative Commons Attribution-Share Alike 4.0 International license
- Link to the material: https://commons.wikimedia.org/wiki/File:Tesla_Cybertruck_outside_unveil_modified_by_Smnt.jpg
- Modification: isolated image from background.

Photo description: VW ID.4
- Photo Title: VW ID Crozz, IAA 2017 (1Y7A2031).jpg
- Name of the creator: MB-one
- This photograph is copyrighted
- License notice: Creative Commons Attribution-Share Alike 4.0 International license
- Link to the material: https://commons.wikimedia.org/wiki/File:VW_ID_Crozz,_IAA_2017_(1Y7A2031).jpg
- Modification: isolated image from background.